DANDELION
Child

A Soldier's Daughter

Margaret Allyn Greene Best

MARGARET ALLYN GREENE BEST

Cover and interior design by Monica Nagy, M&N Marketing Group

ISBN-13: 978-1-939472-32-8
ISBN-10: 1-939472-32-6

Printed in the United States of America

Edited and published by LifeStory Publishing,
a division of Writing Your Life
P.O. Box 541527
Orlando, Florida 32854
WritingYourLife.org

First Edition: March 2019

10 9 8 7 6 5 4 3 2

Contents

Acknowledgments

Dandelion Child: A Soldier's Daughter has been ten years in the making. During that time, I have written and rewritten certain chapters as memories floated through my mind. The final book is nothing like the ones written before.

I am indebted to my late Aunt Kathleen, my grandparents, parents, and brother for their take on several of the stories contained within. Encouragement offered by the Miami Writers Group, The Wannabe Writers of The Villages, Florida, and my dear friend Kathleen Schumm is greatly appreciated. Special thanks go to Marion Roach Smith, Michael Greene, Teresa Bruce, and Patricia Charpentier for their assistance in editing as well as to Larry Mound and Monica Nagy for their help designing the book cover.

Writing and editing and even publishing a book is hard work needing many hands, but once that book is published, more work is necessary. I wish to thank my marketing agent Rebecca Ponton for the work completed on my first book, *Unsung Hero*, and her continuing work for *Dandelion Child: A Soldier's Daughter*.

Without the support of family, an author cannot continue, so I wish to acknowledge support given by my husband, Joel Best, sons Keith and Brian, and my daughter, Elizabeth Smith.

Dandelion Child: A Soldier's Daughter

The Cold War Years, 1947–1969

The dandelion is the official flower of the military child.

Dandelion Children

By Margaret Best

Like dandelions blown by the wind,
Military children set down roots wherever they're sent
And thrive among strange and foreign lands
Where new adventures wait.

They are strong, indestructible survivors
Who stand proud and brave among the thorns.
They protect, support, defend, and sacrifice,
Ready to bloom anew.

The Military Brat

By Margaret Best

Born brave and bold
Resilient, responsible, respectful
Adventurous, adaptable, accepting
Traveled, trusted, and tenacious

This book is dedicated to the millions of
military brats, male and female, who have
traveled the world and waited for their
service parents' return.

Introduction
Dandelion Plight,
Dandelion Pride

For as long as the armed forces have been calling men and women to serve their country, children have been raised in the military. I, as a child, never signed on the dotted line enlisting among the ranks of the United States Navy, Army, Air Force, Marines, National Guard or Coast Guard. Nevertheless, I lived a military existence as support for my soldier parent. Mine is a story shared by many yet understood by few.

Since the years of my childhood, the plight of military children has become recognized for its unique challenges. In 1986, Secretary of Defense Casper Weinberger acknowledged April as the Month of the Military Child to honor our sacrifices.

Most people familiar with the phrase *military brat* rightly assume it refers to children raised by military parents. While use of the word *brat* alone in other contexts is less than flattering, we military brats feel as proud of the designation as we are of our serving parents and their commendations. It's hard to say where the term originated, although some scholars believe the first published mention appeared in a book that referred to British Regiment Attached Travelers—B-R-A-T-S—the family members of British army soldiers. Regardless of the way the term came into being, military brats are now recognized as a distinct population.

As early as the 1940s, many associated the endearing term *brat* with the dependent children of officers serving in the United States Army. Today children of both officers and enlisted personnel are known as *brats*. Some assert the acronym means *born rough and ready* while others suggest an army brat is one who is army-born, army-raised, and army-traveled.

The United States military active-duty troops counted 1,340,533 people in 2015 — the smallest active-duty force since 2001. However, those personnel brought 2.5 million dependents with them into service. This constituted less than 0.04% of the overall US population. However, with the recent wars and national recognition, some have estimated that about one-third of the general population has a direct connection with someone in the military, and virtually everyone has an indirect relationship.

Military families live in our neighborhoods; their children attend our schools. Civilian families and individuals can learn much from them. Building and sustaining healthy, resilient, and thriving military children and families will bring benefits not just to them but to a lot of civilian Americans. The military family is the American family.

Today's dependent families, including their children, deal with additional stresses. They face frequent deployments of uniformed parents sent into war zones with the possibility they will return injured — or perhaps never. Overall demographics have changed. With more single-parent households, as well as the increasing need for dual employment, many families face economic hardship.

Luckily, both civilian and military organizations have developed programs to help military families facing these difficulties. There is more support available today than ever before, but more is needed.

My story explores my memories of how I became who I am while growing up as a child of the military — an army brat — during the Cold War years from 1947 through 1969, when I became a military bride. Even though as an adult I live in a civilian world, I hold to my military past. The values I've shared with my military brat peers — both then and now — include resilience, resourcefulness, adaptability, service and sacrifice, pride, independence, respect, strength, and perseverance. This story may seem outdated, but the strengths I developed and the challenges I overcame are much the same as those faced by today's military children.

We brats—and dandelions also—share unique trials. The answer to a simple question like "Where are you from?" can be frustrating. Making friends quickly is common, but keeping them over time and distance is more difficult. Planning future vacations, celebrations, or moves becomes a source of frustration; we always wonder what may happen to uproot them.

Yet, even when we're uprooted, military brats grow strong and hardy as we're transported into unfamiliar climates, cultures, and communities. We are as much at the mercy of our enlisted or commissioned parents' orders as are dandelion seeds that must follow the whims of wind, whether they're sent into the sky by a delighted child's gentle breath or a high-pressure gale. Wherever we land, we learn to thrive.

This is the story of one such dandelion who is—and always will be—a soldier's daughter.

ONE

From Now to Then

Florida and New York (2018-1947)

Mannequins dressed in various green, white, and blue uniforms of the United States Army, Navy, Air Force, Coast Guard, and Marines inspire a sense of pride and sorrow as I enter a newly created building in The Villages, Florida. Patrons and visitors mill about viewing the paraphernalia of war and peace. I take a deep breath and finger a brass plaque that says, "We give a heartfelt thanks to those who donated to the Eisenhower Recreation Center." Fingering further, I find my name, Peggy Best.

I turn left toward the Douglas MacArthur Room, looking at glass cases where I chose to place emblems of my father's life after his death. I spy his Florida ex-POW license plate number—*001*—and then his 88th Division license plate behind three small flags: two official black-and-white POW-MIA flags surrounding the red, white, and blue Stars and Stripes.

I smile, walking across the room to a large display holding my grandfather's, father's, and brother's medals. Each time I visit, I feel close to Daddy, my unsung hero. As a child of a soldier during the Cold War, I still carry the love, pride, fear, loneliness, and values developed during my nomadic childhood. My husband, a Vietnam veteran and also a child of the military, holds these same values.

Like dandelions, we have learned to survive under different and difficult conditions.

My husband and I visited my parents in 2002 for a Veterans Day Parade in downtown Orlando. Daddy's Veterans of Prisoners of War group, which numbered only seven, took the thirty-eighth position.

Five Marchetti Mavericks flew overhead in perfect formation. Groups of old and young men and women, dressed in the uniforms of the United States Army, Marines, Air Force, and Navy—and children in Boy and Girl Scouts' uniforms—awaited their marching call. Bands competed as they practiced their tunes. Male, and the occasional female, voices counted cadence, and a camel transported in a school bus grumbled. Old soldiers chatted about times past as they waited for the start of the parade.

"Let's go." Our driver, a retired petty officer, helped my father and my husband sit atop the flaming red Camaro while I settled into the front seat. *This is going to be a fantastic parade. I wish I could jump out and watch each group march by as I have at every army post where we've lived, but my place today is here, supporting my father.*

"Next, we welcome veterans who were captured and held prisoner during the Second World War, Korea, or Vietnam," the loudspeaker

Lt. Col. Joel E. Best and Major Albert V. Greene

barked. "They endured deplorable conditions and sometimes torture during their months or years in captivity. Let us give the Orlando Chapter of Prisoners of War our thanks and continued support."

Our escort put his Camaro into motion. Daddy—Major Albert V. Greene, United States Army, ex-POW and veteran of WWII, Korea, and Vietnam—sat proudly atop the car. I remembered Daddy in many Veterans Day parades in New York City dressed in uniform and marching with his father, Sergeant Patrick Greene, a decorated veteran of the Great War. I grinned toward Daddy but shook my head. *Dad's getting older. His memory is fading. His health is good, but his mind is slipping. This may be his last parade.*

That day was my husband's first parade since his return from Vietnam in 1968. Joel—Lieutenant Colonel Joel E. Best, United States Army—sat uncomfortably beside my father. Like many other Vietnam veterans, his return from this unpopular and divisive war was not a happy one. He attended in support of his father-in-law.

At each turn along the parade route, an announcer read the same script: "Next, we welcome..."

Children cheered and waved miniature flags. Mothers, fathers, and children clapped and shouted, "Thank you!"

A man in a dress blue US Marine uniform snapped to attention and saluted. Farther down the road, more men saluted. Daddy sat straighter, and Joel smiled. They returned salutes. I felt proud yet humbled by the crowd's welcome.

More than a decade earlier, the United States had invaded Iraq during a conflict called Desert Storm. That conflict had continued and would eventually include the War on Terrorism. I was not thinking of Afghanistan or Iraq or terrorism during that parade. I simply smiled, honoring my father, my husband, and my brother, Captain Michael Greene, as well as my son, Sergeant Brian Best, who had all served my country. *Lord, let the soldiers fighting today's war be protected. Help their families during their absence.*

"Thank you! We'll never forget," people too young to remember yelled. My heart pounded, and my eyes teared. No, we'll never forget.

Another day we will never forget occurred the year before. At my Miami home on the morning of September 11, 2001, the ring of the telephone woke me.

"Happy birthday." My husband's serious voice reached over the phone lines from Mexico. "Are you awake?"

"Not exactly," I whispered, confused as to why he called in the morning when he was due home that night. I yawned and looked at the clock. It read 9:15.

"They bombed New York," Joel said.

My eyes popped open. "You've got to be kidding."

"Turn on the TV. Two airplanes hit the Twin Towers in New York City."

Not believing this could happen, I quipped, "They didn't have to do that for my birthday." I didn't want to believe him. "Fireworks would have been fine."

Joel chuckled softly and said, "Well, happy birthday."

I sat up, wide-awake. "Are we at war?" I asked.

"I don't know," my husband said. "Turn on the television. The president should be speaking soon. I'll try to get home as soon as possible."

I spent the entire day glued to the television, crying, praying, weeping, and watching the destruction. I worried and questioned as I realized these television scenes were not fiction but real life—and death—happening in my country.

As Joel had said, two jetliners flew into the Twin Towers in New York, causing them to crumble. Another jet burst into the Pentagon in Washington, DC, and a fourth crashed in a field in Pennsylvania after passengers on board fought back against hijackers while leaving cell phone messages of courage and desperation.

That day, thousands of innocent American men, women, and children died. *Why? How could this have happened here? Who is the mastermind behind this? Are we at war? Against whom? Will my son be recalled to fight in a foreign land, or will there be fighting here in the United States of America? What can I do?*

This beginning of terrorism for the United States would forever be referred to as 9/11.

Birthdays should not be celebrated this way.

On the evening of my birthday in 2001, my parents called just as my son, Brian, and I ate a slice of cake from his birthday dinner the night before. Joel and I had planned our son's birthday for September 10th because I didn't want to share mine with anyone. That sounded ludicrous later since my birthday became shared with many people in New York and Washington—but as an unhappy remembrance.

"Happy birthday," Dad said as always.

"Thank you, but it's really not that happy today," I replied.

"I know. Where's Joel?" Dad asked.

"In Mexico. He can't get a flight out."

"He will. Don't worry."

"How is this going to affect Brian's status in the marines?" Mother asked.

"He says he's served his time. He's not in the active reserve, but he tells me that he will go to get whoever did this if he's asked."

"That's how I feel," Dad stated. "But I don't think they'll take a seventy-eight-year-old veteran."

We spoke briefly about other family members still in the service. As I laid my head on my pillow that night, awful pictures of death and destruction, hate and evil filled my mind. I became fifty-four years old that day, shared a piece of cake with my son, and worried about the future of our world.

In response to this terrible attack, the government grounded all flights into and out of the country and closed our borders. Not able to return to Miami from Mexico for several days, Joel called each night telling me of his attempts to get home. He and a coworker planned various ways to enter the United States during this emergency. They booked small-plane seats from Mexico City to a border town where they hoped to cross into Texas. From El Paso, they would rent a car and drive east, possibly to my daughter's home in Houston.

After Joel explained his plan, I wondered if he and his coworker could get back into the States. *Of course, they have their passports and are American citizens, but suppose the borders stay closed and they can't get in.*

Everything stopped.

I lived in a state of uncertainty, shock, and outrage. *Are Americans in danger worldwide? Are we safe in our own country? When will Joel get home?*

On Saturday, September 14, 2001, as Joel and his friend were about to embark on their adventure, the flying ban lifted. Joel, already at the airport, took the first seat out of Mexico City directly to Miami.

The world soon learned a well-financed Saudi Arabian man, Osama bin Laden, was responsible for the attacks. President George W. Bush declared a war on terrorism, and the United States invaded Afghanistan in Operation Enduring Freedom. Americans came together. Civilians supported our soldiers while protesting politics. Soldiers and civilians on both sides died. The families of soldiers suffered. Medals were awarded.

Shock gave way to anger. Flags appeared everywhere. Americans wanted reasons, action, and justice.

Many years before 9/11, an obscure blurb of just four lines appeared in the local Peekskill, New York, newspaper announcing births on Thursday, September 11, 1947. Only a handful of people noticed. My grandmother, Mabel Purdy, cut that section from the paper and pasted it into a pink baby book she had purchased for her daughter, Evelyn.

According to records in the baby book, I weighed six pounds, eleven ounces at birth and measured nineteen inches in length. Old black-and-white photos of my early years present a plump, happy child in the arms of or standing beside a pretty, dark-haired, smiling woman who was my mother, Evelyn Purdy Greene, and a handsome, thin, happy man, my father, Albert Greene.

My nose turned up like a pug's, so my uncle Robert Purdy nicknamed me "Puggy." Grandpa Syd Purdy and Uncle Robert called me "Puggy Geen." My birth certificate showed my name as Margaret Allyn Greene, so how did I get the nickname of Peggy? And why was my middle name Allyn?

Grandma Mabel explained it to me. "Margaret was your father's mother's name, so you are named after her. Allyn comes from the combination of your father's name, Albert, and your mother's name, Evelyn. Al and Lyn. But I have no idea why people named Margaret are often called Peggy."

My father worked in New York City while my mother stayed at home. Dad remained active in the US Army Reserve after the Second World War. My parents and I lived with Grandma Mabel and Grandpa Sydney in the house Grandma called the Purdy Mansion and Mother called the Big House. Dandelions must have grown on the lawn.

TWO

The Big House

New York (1947-1951)

I loved the Big House on Lafayette Avenue in Peekskill, New York.

At first, my parents and I lived in two rooms originally built for my mother's grandmother off the living area of the Big House. After my first birthday, in 1948 we moved from there to Maspeth for a brief time and then to Massapequa. But after my fourth birthday, we returned to the Big House and lived in the upstairs space where my mother and her brothers had their bedrooms. A kitchen was installed there.

The Big House

As a little girl, I entered this section of the house by a long wooden staircase up the side of the home. The sweet smell of cherries and apples along with the happy feel of sunshine made me smile. While climbing up the steps, I'd stop, pick a round, red cherry from the tree that grew at the base of the staircase, and plop it past my lips. I'd scrape its sweet juice into my mouth while plucking the pit between my teeth. Then, when I reached the top of the stair, I'd drop that pit, watch it hit the ground below, and wonder if a tree would grow there like in "Jack and the Beanstalk."

Grandma Mabel and Grandpa Sydney lived downstairs. Grandma remembered her cousins, aunts, uncles, and all the people in the neighborhood gathered together on weekends over several years helping build the Big House. That's why she called it the Purdy Mansion. The Purdy family owned the house, but the plot of ground on which it stood was owned by the family at the top of the hill. My mother and the girl at the top of the hill became lifelong friends.

"It took a long time to build," Grandma Mabel said. "Oh, it was cold in the winter. I recall we were working on the outside wall of one of the rooms when I went into labor with one of the boys." Grandma hissed through her teeth, contemplating. "Probably Robert. They put a blanket over the eaves for privacy, and then the midwife came, and the baby was born." She giggled.

"There was always a big party on the weekends when the family gathered together to work on the house," my mother, Evelyn Purdy Greene, said. "Every night ended with a conga line." Mother's face became dreamy. "We would conga and conga and..."

During an interview, Mother gave me a little more information on what life was like during her growing up years. Life was not fun and games while she grew up on the land she termed *half farm and half not*.

"We didn't work the land. Daddy" — Mother said, meaning my grandfather, Syd Purdy — "worked as a boiler man at Valeria Home. We had three horses, some chickens, and a few pigs." Then, her mood grew pensive. "I couldn't ride the horse because I was a girl. But when they needed someone to play baseball, I became the catcher, so why couldn't I ride the horse?"

My mother said the Great Depression didn't affect them much. My grandfather continued working, and Grandma Mabel and the children tended a small garden where they grew tomatoes and squash. Mother's job was to collect eggs from the chicken coop.

"I remember one day," Mother continued, "I stopped to play. I was carrying my spelling book home to do some homework. I put the book on the ground and ran to play. When I returned to get the book, I discovered that the goat had eaten it. I had to pay for that book." The replacement copy stayed with our family for years.

Years later, after the Second World War, when Mother was a young woman, Daddy's reserve unit trained at Camp Smith at the base of Bear Mountain, fifteen miles from the town of Peekskill. He and his friend, John, often walked to Rose's Bar. From there, they took the bus or hiked into town. Daddy said:

I believe it was in June of 1946 when John and I walked into Mario's Pizza Parlor there in Peekskill. Mario's was a place where we could sit and talk over pizza and meet girls.

I walked over to the jukebox and put a coin in for some record—I don't remember which one. I looked across the room and saw your mother and her friend.

I said to John, "I think I'll go over there and ask that girl to dance."
John said, "Which one?"
I said, "The good-looking one. And you go ask the other one."
Daddy shook his head and grinned.
Then John said, "I don't want to."
And I said, "She's not that bad."
But John said, "No, I don't mean that. It's just that I can't dance."
Daddy's story ended here, but he did walk across the dance floor and approach my mother. "Hello," he said. "May I have this dance?"
"But I don't know you," Mother answered.
"I'm Al. And you are?" he replied.
Mother giggled, took his hand, said, "Evelyn," and moved to the floor where they danced the jitterbug. They did a mean jitterbug.

Al visited Evelyn at the Big House on Lafayette Avenue. There, they talked in the parlor. He often stayed for supper and ate with her entire family—my grandmother Mabel and grandfather Syd, my uncle Robert, and my uncle Richard.

Evelyn was not Catholic, but she agreed to marry Al in the Catholic church in Peekskill, New York, on October 16, 1946. We would celebrate their fiftieth wedding anniversary in Orlando, Florida.

Marriage of Albert Greene and Evelyn Purdy 1946

Al, my father, Albert V. Greene, was born and raised in Greenpoint, Brooklyn, New York City. His father and mother, my grandpa Patrick Greene and my grandma Margaret Hock Greene, lived on Engert Avenue in what was called a *railroad apartment*. Their third-floor home consisted of a long run of rooms with two windows, one on each end. They entered the kitchen and walked through to the first bedroom and then the second and on into the living area with a bathroom stuck between the kitchen and first bedroom. There were no partitions except for the bathroom area.

Daddy had an older sister named Kathleen and two older brothers, James and Patrick. Aunt Kathleen told me Albert was the only one of the children their parents had to tie into the pram. He never stayed still.

My father spoke to me about early memories of living in Greenpoint from about 1928 until around 1942. Daddy went to Saint Cecelia's Parochial School for eight years. "All my teachers were really good. They were all people we really admired even at an early age," he said. "We were always very obedient."

Daddy remembered that his first-grade teacher, Mrs. Lafont, wore knee-high boots with laces that crisscrossed in front, but he recalled different memories of another teacher:

I don't remember which grade I was in, but I remember Mrs. Bealer. She would say, "All right, class. Now we're going to do our multiplication tables."

We'd recite our tables, while she walked around class carrying a large and very heavy ruler.

"Albert, what is six times six?" she'd say.

"Well, oh...uh...I don't know," I would say.

"What do you mean? Didn't you do your homework last night? Stick out your hand." Whack. *"Six...times...six...is...thir...ty...six."*

And if you didn't know it after that, you had to turn your hand over and get hit on the knuckles. Boy, that hurt.

Don't ask me what six times seven is, but I'll never forget six times six is thir-ty-six.

All four Greene children attended Saint Cecelia's Parochial School. They, like others, started first grade and stayed with the same group of students through eighth grade. "We got to know all the kids and became good friends," Daddy said.

You can take the boy out of the city, but you cannot take the city out of the boy. After living all over the world and retiring in Orlando, Florida, Daddy always considered his hometown as Greenpoint in Brooklyn, New York.

Most of our family, if not all, have fled New York City, but whenever Daddy met anyone from Brooklyn, he told stories about his childhood—like when he played stickball in the street. Daddy's brother, Patrick, was a *two-sewer man.* "That," Daddy said, "means Pat could hit the ball two blocks down the street."

My concept of home is different from either of my parents'.

"Where are you from?" people ask when first introduced. Most folks respond with where they were born or where they lived most of their childhood.

To me, home has been wherever I hang my hat, as my father used to say. My response is, "I'm an Army brat. I'm from everywhere and nowhere."

In 1947, I was born in New York, and I moved three times before second grade. In 1955, my brother was born at Schofield Barracks, Oahu, Hawaii. Then, we moved to Fort Devens in Massachusetts, to Fort Benning in Georgia, and back to New York. Later, we lived on three different posts in Germany, where I graduated from high school in 1965. In between these major moves, we stayed in various temporary quarters on different posts.

What was it like having to move often? Not so bad. I thought everybody relocated often as I did. After all, when I was a small child during the Cold War in the military, each post was like living in a small town.

Everything—including grocery stores we called commissaries and department stores we called post exchanges—existed on each post. Every base community established its own medical clinic or hospital, library, swimming pool, teen club, school, snack bar, Officers Club, and NCO Club. Every chapel on base catered to all religions. The movie theater, veterinary clinic, class VI liquor store, and education/craft house catered exclusively to patrons carrying military identification cards.

We lacked for nothing, except perhaps a sense of permanence, closeness to relatives, and everlasting friends. Like the dandelion, we learned to put down roots wherever we landed.

THREE

Training for War

New York and Elsewhere (1950–1952)

"You ran away with the boy next door," Grandma Mabel told me. My mother's mother and I shared many secrets and remained close until her death in 1985. "But when you got to the corner, he became scared and returned home. You kept right on walking."

I don't remember any boy next door, yet as I grew older, there seemed always a boy next door with whom I wished to run. We had already moved from the Big House to Maspeth, New York, and then to Massapequa. Daddy worked at Trunds Meat Packing and later at an aviation plant in the city. He also trained soldiers on weekends in the United States Army Reserve. In those days,

Four-year-old Peggy

mothers stayed home and watched each other's kids. Laundry hung on lines out back, and children played outside. My mother, like most housewives of the time, remained home. I was four years old.

My memory of the incident differed from what Grandma Mabel spoke of. I was lost and couldn't find my way back home. And I was crying.

Being careful to stay on the sidewalk and not cross the street—because I was not allowed to do so—my baby steps stomped as I thought, *I can go wherever I want and do whatever I want, and I can walk on the sidewalk forever and ever. Jimmy can go home—but not me. I'm not scared. Nothing will happen to me.*

I turned the corner onto a major thoroughfare and continued marching along, fueled by the sweet scent of independence and adventure. Cars drove by but did not stop. As I passed a red fire hydrant on the side of the road, my step slowed, and my empty tummy growled.

I had been walking for what seemed like a long time. My little legs felt tired. Nothing looked familiar. *Which way should I go?* Tears welled up in my eyes and spilled over. *Mommy's going to be mad*, I thought, but I kept walking.

"Are you lost, little girl?" a man's voice said. "Would you like me to take you home?"

"I'm not allowed to speak to strangers," I said and kept walking. "I want Daddy." My heart pounded as my pace slowed. The man stepped alongside. Tears dribbled down my cheeks as I sniffed, trying to stifle the fear of being lost. I would not stop.

"Peggy," the man said. "Your mother is worried. She called me, so I could take you home."

"Mommy will be mad." I looked at the man. He wore a blue uniform.

"Mommy's not mad. She's worried," the policeman said. "I know what. Let's make a phone call, and I'll take you home in the squad car. Would you like that?" My tears dried as we walked hand in hand toward a wooden phone booth like the one Clark Kent used when he changed into Superman in the comics Daddy read to me.

When we arrived home, Mommy hugged me, and Daddy hugged me, and then the policeman left. I often tried my mother's patience with my rather independent streak.

"I'll never forget it," said Aunt Kathleen, who never forgets anything and recalled details I didn't. "You didn't run away. You just wandered off. I was riding with the police when we saw you walking alone down the street. The policeman called your name, and you said, 'I'm not allowed to speak to strangers,' and just kept on walking. So, it was decided that we'd go back to let your mom know that you were okay. An officer walked beside you until you were ready to go home."

Running away, either physically or psychologically, became my way of dealing with highly stressful situations. Shortly after I ran away, in 1952, Daddy prepared for war.

Mommy no longer smiled, and Daddy wore a uniform. The United States had gone to war in a faraway place called Korea. They needed Daddy to help out, but before he could leave for Korea, he had to complete more training. We moved to Fort Dix, New Jersey, and then returned to Peekskill while Daddy went away for TDY or *temporary duty*.

One memory stands out for me—how we determined I needed eyeglasses.

Mommy, Daddy, and I had just moved to Fort Dix. We lived in a wooden building called *the barracks* with lots of other families. Every day, I waited outside on our hill for Daddy to come home.

When will he get here? I anxiously asked myself. *All the other cars have come up already. Everybody's father is home now. Where's Daddy?*

I ran up and down the hill, keeping an eye out for any vehicles with men wearing uniforms. Several parked in spots far below my hill. *All the cars have men in uniform in them. How can I tell which one is Daddy?*

A man waved. I waved back, not certain as to the man's identity. I stayed on the hill while the man who waved came closer. I shook all over.

"What's wrong?" Daddy asked.

"I couldn't see who you were. I was afraid it wasn't you," I answered.

Daddy scooped me up and carried me into our rooms in the barracks. Soon after that, I wore glasses.

It may not seem like an earth-shattering experience to anyone else, but to me, having to wear glasses was traumatic from day one. Being nearsighted meant I could not see things far away, but what I saw was not fuzzy. Unless I had to discern something like faces or letters, I could see well enough without my glasses. But astigmatism made reading letters difficult. Sometimes the letter *o* turned into the letter *a*, or *c* looked like *o*.

Few other children in school wore glasses.

"Here comes Four-Eyes," kids taunted.

It never occurred to me to come back with a good response like "Better to see you with, my dear," so I tended to hide the glasses whenever possible. I'd started pre-primary school in Wrightstown, New Jersey, but stayed there only a few weeks. I did poorly in reading readiness and number recognition.

Then, we moved back to Peekskill where we lived on Orchard Street.

I must have worn my glasses like a good little girl because the next kindergarten report card from Oakside Elementary School indicated that I improved. However, Mrs. Durkee wrote: "Peggy is showing the effect of her three changes during the first year of school. This will work itself out when she develops a feeling of permanence."

The only permanence for military children was impermanence. Situations changed without notice. I lived in five different homes before my fifth birthday.

Whenever possible, Mommy and I followed Daddy wherever the army stationed him. After the three moves we made during kindergarten, we moved again from Peekskill, New York, to Missouri and back to Peekskill during my first-grade year. I learned to adapt quickly. I began to feel the insecurity associated with permanent change.

I started biting.

"Peggy, you must not bite," Mommy scolded. "It hurts when you bite. Would you like someone to bite you?"

I don't think anybody bit me back, but I do remember being led to the sink—kicking and screaming—so I could bite on a bar of soap. I guess the idea was that I would subconsciously relate my biting someone else with the awful taste of lye that made my mouth pinch together in sympathy. It must have worked because I haven't bitten anyone for years now.

My mother also used soap as a weapon in the war on words.

I was never without something to say. I learned early that *sticks and stones will break your bones, but names will hurt forever.*

No one in my family used profanity. We had no television in the house, and the radio was censored. When I felt frustrated trying to get attention for one thing or another, I learned using certain words in a loud, demanding manner shocked the adults around me. I used this tactic a few times—until Mommy lost her patience. She led me away to the sink and washed my mouth out with soap. She must have thought my words would become clean if the soap got to them. Instead, I learned to mumble my words to keep them unheard. I'm still a mumbler.

While we lived on Orchard Street in Peekskill, Daddy attended OCS, or Officer Candidate School, at Fort Benning, Georgia. With him gone, I spent time wandering around Peekskill. I explored nooks, crannies, and alleys, and I climbed up and down hills, walking everywhere with my mother and my imaginary puppy.

I had a lot of imaginary friends. In fact, I often made up stories about those friends, leading Mommy to think I did not tell the truth. To me, though, the stories I made up were as real as if they had been true.

I felt happy in Peekskill. Grandma Mabel took me to the Big House, where I could play on my swing or watch *Howdy Doody* on the black-and-white television set. I also played dominos and checkers, cut out paper dolls, and made my stories come true— at least to me. I enjoyed singing songs like "Here Comes Suzie Snowflake" and "I've Been Working on the Railroad" while watching the little bouncing ball on the TV screen. Betty Boop, Lamb Chop, and Bozo the Clown were my companions. Sometimes, I played with my cousin Susan, who lived upstairs in the Big House.

In 1952, we moved from Orchard Street in Peekskill to Fort Leonard Wood, Missouri, where Daddy received additional training. Now a second lieutenant, he prepared for his second war while my mother and I continued learning how to adapt to continual change, which included making new friends.

We lived in a duplex on post housing at Fort Leonard Wood. I rode a school bus every morning for first grade and played outside after school. I was the youngest on our block and, as I recall, the only girl.

Cars drove down the street in front of my house on their way home. A group of older boys gathered beside the road and organized a game. One boy yelled, "Run!" while another dashed across the street before a car passed by, and everybody laughed.

"Can I play?" I asked.

"Sure," a boy said. "Run!"

I ran and made it to the other side of the street. Everybody clapped, and then, one at a time, the boys ran across the road.

Cars kept coming. The boys took turns running from one side of the street to the other while playing chicken with the cars. When they all reached the other side, I stood alone across the way.

"Come on, Peggy. You can make it. Run!"

I ran.

BANG.

The man's horrified eyes behind his steering wheel looked big.

The soldier who hit me carried me into the house and placed me on the sofa. People crowded into our living room. Mother hovered around the room. Her face looked pale. People whispered. My eyes opened, but I felt dazed and confused. *What happened?*

Mommy kept talking to me, but I couldn't hear what she was saying. *How come all these people are here, but Daddy is not? Where is Daddy?*

Then, I saw him walk through the doorway. "Daddy," I said, "I ran into a car."

Everybody breathed a sigh of relief. I was fine, but I learned cars were mightier than little girls.

Shortly afterward, we moved again.

This time, we returned from Missouri to Peekskill and lived in the same house in which Grandma Mabel grew up on Paulding Street across from Oakside Elementary School. It was November, and I was in first grade. I had adapted to five different houses, three separate schools, and many unfamiliar playmates in a short span of time, but a more difficult change loomed ahead.

FOUR

First Deployment

New York (1952–1953)

I was three years old when, on June 25, 1950, North Korean forces crossed the dividing line between North and South Korea. In defense of the South, the United States joined the fighting under the banner of the United Nations. By the time Daddy arrived there, millions of soldiers and civilians had been killed. The year between 1952 and 1953 passed with difficulty for both my mother and me. At age six, I only understood that Daddy had to go away.

"Why do you have to go?" Daddy and I sat on the bed in the big room downstairs in the house Aunt Evelyn Owen owned at 853 Paulding Street across from Oakside Elementary School in Peekskill, New York.

"It's my job, Peggy. I'm a soldier," he said.

The Greene Family—
Mommy, Daddy, Peggy

23

"But you can stay here and be a soldier. I don't want you to go."
I had entered first grade in my fourth school, and I lived close to
Grandma Mabel. Life could have been perfect except for this one
thing. "Please don't go. You might get killed."

"I have to go," he said. "Don't worry."

Daddy kissed me, joined my mother on the porch, and got into a
taxi. I watched through the window as he left.

Feeling lost and abandoned, I did not understand what was happening or how long he would be gone. My nighttime dreams often
involved flying in a helicopter, searching the ground for dead bodies.
Then, the dream changed to looking for Daddy, who was lost.

A cease-fire went into effect on July 27, 1953. Shortly afterward,
the 14th Regiment of the 25th Infantry Division moved to Camp
North Star in South Korea, where an intensive training program
commenced. Daddy wore silver lieutenant bars and worked at
headquarters helping set up the Demilitarized Zone, the DMZ, at
the thirty-eighth parallel. Many years later, I asked my father about
his tour in Korea. "It was cold," he said. "I was in transit when the
fighting stopped." That was the only information he gave.

Meanwhile, back at home, my mother worked as a girl Friday at an
electric light supply company in downtown Peekskill. I walked across
the street every morning to Oakside Elementary School, and Mommy
walked to her office on Washington Street. After school, I visited the
elderly woman who lived on the floor above us in our house.

"Come on up," Old Lady Upstairs said. "We can have a chat
until your mother comes home. I'll make butterfly sandwiches."
First, she sliced off the crusts from two pieces of Wonder Bread.
Then, she spread them with peanut butter and cut the sandwich into
four diagonal sections. She arranged each section sideways, picked
one up, and pretended it fluttered from the plate into her mouth. I
loved butterfly sandwiches.

I didn't like school. I thought the principal had a big paddle, and
if your teacher sent you to the office, the principal would put you on
a long table—like a conveyer belt—where he would beat you. I was
called to the office once. I don't remember why, but I felt petrified.

Fortunately, the principal turned out to be a nice man. He greeted me at the door, smiled, invited me to sit, and talked about how pleased he was that I attended his school. "I know your father is away," he said. "If you want to talk, just let your teacher know."

My teacher was a kind woman who taught us how to make candied apples. Once, however, I forgot to put my pants on under my snowsuit. When I got to school, she insisted I take off my snow pants. Scared, I fought her, but the snowsuit came off, and I was in my underwear.

My report card noted that I had difficulty controlling my temper.

Often, my mother arranged for me to join my friend Robin after school. One day, while Robin and I walked to her three-story home on the hill, she and I decided we needed money for something. I knew Mommy kept her change in a jar. She hid it behind the ledge at the top of the tall mirror on our chiffonier. She also kept our apartment key above the front doorjamb.

"Just climb up and get it," Robin said. We'd stopped walking and stood in front of my house on the way to hers. "I dare you."

Peggy, first grade in Peekskill, New York

I felt guilty and scared, but Robin dared me, so I climbed onto the closest stair, stood on tiptoe, strained to reach above our door, shoved my finger toward the key, and slid my palm across until the key clinked onto the porch. Still frightened—but unwilling to back down—I entered our apartment while Robin stood watch at the front door.

Inside, I climbed on top of the high dresser and stretched until my hand found the forbidden jar filled with coins Mommy saved for incidentals like lunch and milk. I don't remember how much money I took, but I do remember her anger when she found it missing.

My mother and I did not see eye to eye, and since I noticed tension between her and her mother, I believed mothers and daughters just naturally did not get along. Parents gave instruction, and children did what they were told, but my mother and I argued constantly. When she became frustrated with my willfulness, she used a green knitting needle as her switch.

Mommy punished me every morning for things I was going to do wrong—and again in the evening for all those things I did do wrong. I was always getting into trouble. "I remember picking you up on Saturday and seeing your leg bright red with welts," Grandma Mabel told me.

Whenever things got out of hand at home, Grandma Mabel appeared at the door and took me to the Big House where I played with cousin Susan. I often spent the night, even when I had school the next day.

Grandma and I ate at a special Chinese restaurant and talked and giggled like good friends. We shopped at Genung's, the A&P, and the five-and-dime, where we enjoyed tuna club sandwiches and chocolate soda. Grandma Mabel became my best friend. We shared a special bond, and I wanted to be the same kind of grandma she was.

Grandma Mabel's sister, Evelyn, and my mother, who happened to share the name, were good friends. Aunt Evelyn lived in Mount Kisco, New York. Her house held sturdy, all-wood furniture; beautiful crystal chimes; large, Colonial-looking clocks; lovely china; and a most precious, antique, leather-bodied doll. She wore an Early American dress and had a hand-painted porcelain face and sat on a small wicker chair in the corner.

I was not allowed to play with her, but I spent hours looking at her and creating stories about her. At six years old, I decided I wanted to collect treasures such as this. I hoped Aunt Evelyn would give that doll to my mother, and then Mommy would give it to me, but that didn't happen. Sadly, Aunt Evelyn died without preparing a will, and all her marvelous antiques and historical knickknacks disappeared from the family.

Since then, I have not found any doll as special, except the doll my father's father, Grandpa Patrick Greene, won for me. During one of the visits my mother and I made to Greenpoint while Daddy was away, Grandpa Patrick and I took the subway to Coney Island. Grandpa Patrick held my hand, and we walked toward a boardwalk so we could swim under it. On our way, we passed a carnival-type kiosk where a ceramic Snow White doll stood fifteen inches tall and glistened in the sun.

"Grandpa, she's beautiful." I pointed to the doll.

Grandpa paid the man, lifted a long hammer, and struck at something that caused a ball to zip up toward a huge bell. I felt so excited I jumped up and down and clapped my hands. After Grandpa made several tries, the bell rang, and he handed me the most beautiful ceramic Snow White doll that ever existed. Her dress was yellow, and the bird on her shoulder was blue. I kept that doll through many moves. After I married, movers dropped her, and she shattered. I felt as if my entire childhood had crumbled with her. Even glue could not fix her.

Dolls weren't my only interest in those days. I thoroughly enjoyed dancing.

After school and on weekends, my mother and I walked downtown to the fire station; I took tap dance lessons in the upstairs room next door. When it came time for the recital, I felt prepared. Mommy and Grandma sat in the audience, and Grandma had her ever-present Brownie camera poised and ready.

The voice of Patti Page sang out, "How much is that doggie in the window?" and I tapped on stage as part of the line. *Tap...tap...tap...*

Oh, no. My hat is falling off. Terrified, I fumbled with my cap as I continued tapping.

The audience laughed and clapped, but I fell over myself trying to set my hat back onto my head. The experience traumatized and embarrassed me so much that I became physically ill before any other recital. Nevertheless, I continued to perform. As I grew up, I danced the hula before audiences and played the piano despite feeling fraught with anxiety over each performance.

Although playing with my friends and my cousin and taking tap lessons after school filled many afternoons while missing my daddy, I yearned for a live dog to replace my imaginary one. After much begging, including showing Mommy the puppies available in the pet store I passed on the days I walked to her office, she finally gave in to my wish.

Spotty—a cute little beagle—and I ran up and down the hills of Peekskill. We played on the playground and chased each other up the big hill to my mother's friend's house. The woman's son Johnny and I played cops and robbers while Spotty trotted along. Johnny became my first forever boyfriend. Mommy called it puppy love.

While attending school, we tied Spotty to the fence post in front of the house. Since we lived directly across the street from the school, I often left the playground to check on him. This, I learned, was not acceptable. Out came the green switch.

I started second grade in September 1953. My mother kept our black dial telephone on the closet shelf opposite the front door. One afternoon, she was busy in the kitchen when the phone rang. I ran into the hall, jumped up, reached the phone, and heard lots of static. A voice said, "Will you accept a long-distance call from Korea?"

Mommy grabbed the phone from my hand.

"Go into the kitchen while I talk on the phone," she said.

Korea? "I think that's Daddy. I want to talk to him."

"Go. Now." Mommy pointed toward the kitchen.

I went.

My mother took a long time talking on the phone. I sat at the kitchen table, looking out the window at the birds in the trees. When I couldn't stand it any longer, I crept into the hall next to her while she still talked with Daddy. "It's your turn," she said and handed the receiver to me.

There was so much static that I couldn't hear well. "Daddy," I said.

"Yes, honey. Now, listen while I tell you how to use the telephone," Daddy said. "I'm on a radio in the field in Korea. When I say, 'Over,' it is time for you to talk. When you finish talking, you say, 'Over,' and I'll talk. Do you understand? Over."

"Yes. Over."

"I miss you, honey. How are you doing? Over."

"I miss you too, Daddy. When are you coming home?" I waited for Daddy to respond, but he didn't until I said, "Over."

"I can't come home now…but soon…Over."

Screetch…scratch…

"I have a dog, and I go to school and—"

Screetch…scratch…

"Honey, there's so much…static." *Screetch.* "It's hard to hear you." *Scratch.* "I have to hang up now." *Scr…eetch…*"I love you. Out."

The phone went dead. Mommy took the receiver and hung up. "I didn't have enough time to tell him all the stuff I wanted to." I glared up at my mother.

"Daddy had to hang up," she said.

"You took all the time!" I yelled. Mommy turned toward the kitchen while I continued my temper tantrum. "I wanted to talk to Daddy."

That evening, Grandma stopped by and took me to the Big House.

Sometime later, my mother told me we were going to Hawaii to meet Daddy, but first I had to give Spotty to the nice veterinarian. "Why can't we take Spotty with us to Hawaii?"

"He cannot come with us. Only you and I can go to meet Daddy."

"But who will take care of Spotty?"

"The veterinarian will."

"No," I protested. "Robin said the doctor will put Spotty to sleep. I don't want him to go to sleep."

After much discussion, argument, and crying, we decided the doctor would find a good home for my dog and not put him to sleep. With no other options, Mommy and I walked with Spotty on his leash up, over, and down the hills of Peekskill to the veterinarian's office. Walking those blocks seemed like walking the last mile to my execution. The heaviness in my steps gradually crept up into the pit of my tummy and then expanded up through my throat and leaked out from under my eyelids.

Once at the veterinarian's office, I tearfully kissed my dog goodbye and promised him he would be well cared for. When I handed the leash over to the doctor, he gave me a lollipop. A lollipop!

I asked Grandma about Spotty when I visited in 1956. She assured me her friend, the veterinarian, had taken Spotty home with him to live a long and healthy life.

Shortly after relinquishing my dog and packing our belongings, Mommy and I met my father's sister and brother-in-law—Aunt Kathleen and Uncle Whitey—with my cousin Maureen and Grandma Margaret and Grandpa Patrick Greene at the New York International Airport.

"Aren't you excited?" Maureen blurted out. Always bubbly, Maureen never lacked for something to say. "I wish I could go on a big airplane like you. I bet you'll have lots of fun in Hawaii. I bet you'll swim...and...and...Oh, here. I got you this teeny tiny tea set with itty-bitty spoons, so you can use them on the plane when—"

"Okay," Mommy said. "We're ready. Let's go."

Peering through the window of the propeller-driven passenger airplane and mesmerized by the myriad of blinking lights under the midnight sky, my heart raced as we took off—leaving Grandma Mabel and Spotty behind—in search of Daddy, whom I decided had been lost in Korea.

The next morning, we landed in California. We waited a short time before embarking upon a steam-driven ocean liner for the long, two-week trip across the Pacific Ocean to Hawaii.

Back and forth the deck rolled, hour after hour. We steamed across the never-ending deep, blue ocean that made my stomach ache, causing me to throw up in the potty.

We had to wear life jackets just in case the boat should sink like the *Titanic*. Or, if we ran too fast, we might trip and fall overboard into the sea. We'd drown and get eaten up by sharks or maybe even a whale!

My seven-year-old imagination had lots of time to create these nightmares and daydreams. This led to a lifelong fear of water. Only after years of deliberate effort could I, at age fifty-five, float in the swimming pool without fear. While living in Guam, I finally learned to swim—at age sixty-two.

At last, we arrived. My mother and I put on our best dresses and moved with the throng to the side of the ship to watch as we docked in Honolulu, Oahu, in the territory of Hawaii. A crowd—mostly of uniformed soldiers—waited, waved, and shouted. Most had not seen their wives and children for years while they served in Korea.

A band played Hawaiian music. Ladies dressed in colorful muumuus, with brightly colored plumeria flowers adorning their hair, danced a welcome hula.

"Just look over the railing, Peggy. Daddy will be there." Mommy looked pretty. "When you see him, wave, and I will too."

Suddenly shy, ready to cry, I worried. *What if I don't recognize him? I'm wearing my glasses, but I can't see him. Maybe he's still in Korea.* I searched, but I could not find Daddy. *Is he still lost?*

"Look, Peggy. Look." Mommy bent to my face and pointed. "There's Daddy. See him? He's smiling and waving at you."

The Greene family in Hawaii

Daddy rushed to greet us. He put a lei over Mommy's head and kissed her. Then he reached down to me, put a lei over my head, and picked me up. I was back in my hero's arms, and we were in Hawaii together. But my life was about to change in another unexpected way.

FIVE

Aloha

Hawaii (1954–1956)

Daddy served as a second lieutenant in the 25th Tropic Lightning Infantry Division stationed at Schofield Barracks in Oahu, Hawaii. When I visited his company, I played under the coconut tree across from the parade ground. Daddy placed a young soldier or two in charge of me. If I had to go to the restroom, one of the soldiers inspected the toilet—what the military called the *head*—to be sure it was empty and then stood guard at the door until I returned. Sometimes, I visited the kitchen—*mess*—where soldiers who were on kitchen police duty—*KP*—peeled potatoes.

I smiled whenever I heard soldiers count cadence and eagerly watched them practice their drills or run double-time. I mimicked what I saw and learned how to stand at attention, be at ease, salute, and march—*hup, two, three, four.*

I stopped whatever I was doing when the cannon boomed and stood at attention because the garrison flag was being lowered. I wore my dog tags, and, when I got older, I carried my identification card. I was in the army just like Daddy, and I loved it.

I was seven years old.

The army of my youth consisted almost entirely of men who had either volunteered or been drafted into service for a specified number of years. It was set up in what appeared to me to be two separate links that worked together like an interconnected chain where orders passed from top to bottom. Wives and children became family units that conformed to established military codes, rules, regulations, and traditions.

I thought of the army as being like a cake.

I liked cake.

The base—and largest layer—of this army cake consisted of men and their families of enlisted rank from private to master sergeant. Warrant officers and their families comprised a thin midsection, and the top layer consisted of officer-ranked men and their families from second lieutenants to four-star generals—five-star in time of war. A thin layer of civilian frosting, composed of government officials headed by the president of the United States, covered this entire cake structure.

Daddy wore his uniform, left for work every day before I headed to school, and returned home in time for dinner around five after other soldiers lowered the flag. Occasionally, he trained on the Big Island of Hawaii for a week or two, but he always came home. When Daddy was at home, our family spent time together.

We often ate dinner in fine restaurant style at the Officers Club. Happy hour was every Friday, and there were dances every Saturday. During the week, we played bingo, ping-pong, or foosball at the club. Women gathered for their ladies' luncheons, hula lessons, or to play bridge. Children attended classes in crafts, hula dancing, and charm. We held Girl Scout meetings there. The O Club offered a place of retreat.

We swam at the post swimming pool where lifeguards were always on duty. The pool was for officers and their families to use only because it was behind the Officers Club. I think enlisted families swam in another pool. When we were not at home or shopping at the post exchange, commissary, or thrift shop, or playing at the O Club, the bowling alley, or the movie theater, we often drove around the island of Oahu.

During our stay in 1954, 1955, and 1956, the islands of Hawaii were a territory of the United States. The land remained a beautiful paradise, still unspoiled. Few tall buildings and no superhighways marred the views. Everywhere we drove, we saw green mountains or pineapple and sugarcane fields. People wore simple clothing and no shoes.

Folks also played volleyball, surfed, and swam on Waikiki Beach. As the song said, there really were little grass shacks on Waikiki Beach. Daddy played with me in the waves and stood by me with his arms open while I splashed. Sometimes, he took me sailing with a group of his friends. I didn't like going on the boats or wading too far offshore. I didn't know how to swim. I preferred sitting on the beach building sandcastles and creating stories.

Every Sunday after church, Daddy, Mommy, and I drove around the island of Oahu sightseeing. We often stopped at roadside stands to taste the sweet tang of fresh pineapple that grew in the fields. We listened to the radio in the car and sang tunes with Frank Sinatra, Dean Martin, Rosemary Clooney, and Dinah Shore. Mommy also liked to sing while she worked around the house. She sang a song about a pie man who had rhythm in his nursery rhymes. Mommy seemed happy in Hawaii.

Other than the times I spent with Daddy, I don't remember feeling happy in Hawaii. I made few friends and disliked school. I missed Grandma Mabel and remained a stubborn little girl.

I argued constantly with my mother. I also played Mommy against Daddy. When I asked Mommy permission to do something like ride my blue bicycle, she usually said no, so I learned to ask Daddy, who sometimes said yes. Then, I'd tell Mommy, "But Daddy said it was okay," and I'd get my way.

Soon, Mommy and Daddy learned to present a unified front. When I asked Daddy first, he said, "Ask your mother."

Despite those times, my father took extra effort to play with me. I enjoyed riding my brand-new, big-girl, two-wheeler bicycle with his help. Daddy ran beside me on the gravel road in front of our house until I said, "Okay," and he let go.

I balanced and pedaled by myself.

A few times, I fell, but I always got back up and rode on. Eventually, I found friends down the street who also rode bikes.

One family we knew lived in a home by a cove where waves crashed over a rock wall. I wanted to explore that area, but my mother did not permit me to go without an adult. So, my bike-riding friends and I rode together. We always returned before Mommy knew where I had been. I worried the entire way back that I would get into more trouble.

Most times when I was in trouble, it had something to do with bad-mouthing my mother. When Daddy came home from work, I had to apologize. I grew up saying "I'm sorry" for just about everything.

Mommy and Daddy hosted a cocktail party at the house one evening when I was seven. Nobody knew I was in the room until someone saw me lean on the wall and slowly slump to the floor—I had quietly sampled each adult beverage. After that, my parents became more vigilant and introduced me to age-appropriate drinks: Shirley Temple and Roy Rogers on the rocks. A Shirley Temple made by my mother contained a mixture of ginger ale and cherry juice while a Roy Rogers was Coca-Cola and pineapple juice. A plump cherry or an olive topped each. Sometimes, a small umbrella graced my glass.

Our family lived at 67260 Kukea Circle in Waialua next to a Hawaiian family named Takato. We enjoyed many luaus or cookouts at their house after Daddy returned from fishing and crabbing with Mr. Takato. I ran through a sugarcane field with the Takato kids. The canes brushed and scraped against my cheeks. I wore shoes. The Takatos did not.

At school, with the Cold War heating up, children stood outside every morning to say the Pledge of Allegiance. Whenever a siren rang, we sat under our desks. A sign on the wall in each hallway indicated the way to our fallout shelter. We were courting nuclear disaster. I was in the second grade.

It seemed I didn't learn much at that school, but I made a necklace for my mother from brown seeds. My report card showed that I made progress in social behavior and work habits, but I needed to borrow library books and read more. The teacher marked grades with a plus, check, or minus but only in social adjustment, work habits, and health. I received no academic grades. Didn't they teach reading or math?

I loved only one part of our school curriculum: learning the hula. I wore muumuus and flip-flops called *idewa* shoes. I also donned a grass skirt when I danced "The Hukilau Song" and "Little Brown Gal."

Mommy too learned to dance the hula but in the evening at a special place. I enjoyed watching her dance because she looked graceful and pretty.

Peggy and Mommy dancing the hula in
Peekskill, New York, 1956

We moved into our second Hawaiian home in on-post housing at 3160 C GG Area Schofield Barracks on Oahu. Often, coconuts fell onto the ground from the big tree in our front yard. We cut the coconuts open and drank the milk and ate the fruits' meat.

A large, sliding glass door separated our living room from the backyard. Because Schofield Barracks was situated in a tropical rainforest, trees grew thick just beyond our yard. Mommy did not allow me to go into the forest; she said there might be snakes in the trees. I learned later snakes were not indigenous to Hawaii.

At times, I accidentally lost one of my shoes and had to search for it just at the edge of the forest. *Everyone knows that all shoes land in the same place*, I reasoned, so I threw my second shoe into the forest and then quietly searched. I explored in the forbidden area—remaining within eyesight of our house—whenever I thought I could get away with it. This was a constant irritation to my mother. Sometimes, I found both shoes or beautiful flowers—but no snakes. I'd sit on the porch making leis of these flowers. Fortunately, I knew some of the blossoms were poisonous, so I never ate any of them.

Our small, first television set had antennae rabbit ears that needed continual adjustment. Often, the black-and-white show appeared so fuzzy it grew impossible to see. When that happened, Daddy used magic to fix it. He pointed at the set, stomped his foot, and the show either disappeared or came on without fuzz. I thought he did this by some magic only he possessed. He told me much later that stomping on a loose board sometimes moved the antennae just right.

I faithfully watched a children's clown show each day, and I felt overjoyed when I had a chance to attend and be on television. I practiced my funny face every day, all day long. When we visited the studio, I looked around in surprise that the set didn't look like it did on our television. The other children and I lined up to do our funny faces. I tried, but my face didn't come out. Then, the clown had me move on. Despite my disappointment, I had fun going there. That clown remained my idol for a while.

I liked jumping rope, playing jacks, and making up elaborate stories for my paper dolls. Most of the time, I played alone, acting my stories out on a large, outdoor stage built like a log cabin in the playground across the street from our house. I had a big imagination, and sometimes people accused me of lying when I was merely telling a story. Simple things seemed much more exciting with a little embellishment. The imaginary world I built for myself was always clouded gray and fringed with color.

With every move came a new school. During the 1955–56 school year, I attended Mrs. Fujioka's third grade at Schofield School located about five miles from my home. Schofield School had a clinic staffed with a school nurse. Illnesses like smallpox, tuberculosis, and polio were being eradicated. It seemed that I was always getting shots for one thing or another. Fear of the needle clouded my judgment to the point that I often screamed, or worse, before succumbing to the vaccination.

"Boys and girls, line up here and walk down the hall to the clinic," Mrs. Fujioka said. "Your parents have all signed the permission slip for this vaccination. We've discussed the reasons for this shot, but there are so many of us we'll have to wait our turn."

We lined up in the hall and walked in a straight line. My breath quickened as I thought, *I don't want a shot. The needle's so big.* I looked right and left trying to find any way out. *I will not have this shot.*

I darted out of line and down the walkway into the parking lot.

I heard people yelling at me to return, but I kept on going.

The walk home was long and filled with guilt. Tears streamed down my face as I walked the boulevard. *If I walk far enough, I'll fall into the ocean and drown.*

When I arrived home, Mommy was waiting, both angry and worried. When Daddy came, we had a talk, and he took me to the clinic. I received my vaccination.

By the end of grade three, my report—with academic marks of A, B, C, D, or F and personal trait grades of number one, two, or three— showed that I struggled with reading and arithmetic. I received Cs in most subjects except oral English in which I received a B.

Although I should have worn my glasses, I usually lost them or misplaced them. I didn't like reading and couldn't see the chalkboard, but not seeing seemed better than being teased. My class photographs show me as the only white student, or *haole*, in my class and the only one wearing glasses, so kids called me Four Eyes. I did not like school at all, and I hated my glasses.

Second grade class in Hawaii,
Peggy, second row, fifth from the left

Adjusting to so many changes at such an early age was not easy for me. Not yet eight years old, I had moved seven times. Whenever I felt powerless, which happened frequently, I ran away or withdrew into a world of make-believe. My kindergarten teacher in Peekskill had mentioned that behavior would improve when I felt a sense of permanence. But how could military children like me learn to adjust to constant change? Becoming pliable and accepting change carried much more importance than permanence. I slowly developed skills needed for coping with unpredictability.

I enjoyed the repetition of our favorite family outings. We often visited Pearl Harbor on the island of Oahu, where World War II started for the United States on December 7, 1941. And we enjoyed wading on the beach at Waikiki while looking at an extinct volcano named Diamond Head. Volcanoes still erupted on the Big Island of Hawaii, and sometimes the ground moved.

One evening in February 1955, Mommy, Daddy, and I traveled in a small car similar to a Volkswagen. Mommy wore a blue taffeta cocktail dress, Daddy wore his dress blue uniform, and I wore my favorite red polka-dot dress. We were going to a gathering. I sat in the back seat.

"Several volcanoes on the island of Hawaii erupted this morning," a voice on the radio announced. "Be on the lookout for a tsunami."

"What's a tsunami?" I asked.

"Nothing to worry about," Daddy said.

"Where is the water coming from?" I asked, noticing that the streets and lawns were becoming covered with water. The sky was overcast, but there was no rain.

"The ocean waves—but they'll go back out," Daddy replied.

I saw no waves.

Daddy stopped our car in front of a big house and opened the door on Mother's side. Water was everywhere and getting deeper by the minute. Daddy lifted Mommy out of the car and carried her to the front door. He sloshed in ankle-deep water. "Stay in the car. I'll be right back."

I was not frightened. There was no rain and no thunder, but where was all this water coming from? Water entered the car and spilled over its floor. I lifted my feet onto the seat, waiting for Daddy and watching water fill our car. Everything flooded in the short time he was gone. Soon, the water reached my seat.

Where's Daddy? I thought. *The doors are closed, but the water keeps coming into the car.* My eyes widened, but I knew Daddy would return.

He was knee-deep in water when he carried me into the house.

That was certainly an adventure. Our evening was spent in someone's home with lots of other children who were as excited as I. When we left a few hours later, there was no water in the streets at all.

Since all the soldiers returned from Korea at the same time, a mini baby boom blossomed nine months later.

Mommy was pregnant, and I was excited. I wanted a little brother. Actually, I really wanted a big brother, but a little brother would have to do. I crossed my fingers that the baby would be a boy.

I sat with Mommy on the bed discussing names for a little boy. Because my initials were MAG for Margaret Allyn—*Al-* for Albert and *-lyn* for Evelyn—Greene, my brother's initials also had to be MAG: Michael, I decided, and Albert for Daddy. Since we lived in Hawaii, we decided the baby needed a Hawaiian name. We found that *Alapaki* was the closest name to Albert. That's how I named my brother Michael Alapaki Greene. Everyone called him Pahakaloah.

Daddy told a better story. He said, "When looking over the calm surf of Waikiki Beach and across the horizon, you will see a mountain called Diamond Head. There, upon the mountain, is a beautiful jeweled fountain named..." He stopped talking, waiting for people to look at the mountain, and then he said, "Alapaki means Albert in Hawaiian."

During her pregnancy, my mother was often sick. I tried to stay quiet, but I always got into some kind of trouble. My mother and I argued often, and I began to feel like everything was my fault. I wanted so much to be good, but I just was unable to control my temper.

As is typical of every precocious child, I thought I was being treated in an unfair manner, so the only thing I could think of to do was to run away. I ran from school, but I also ran from home whenever I felt overwhelmed. I didn't stay away long because I was really just trying to find Daddy. Running away from my problems in one form or another became a pattern in my life.

My mother's pregnancy was difficult. I remember that she was gone often, and Daddy fed me potato chips and cake for breakfast.

The night of the baby's birth, I lay on a couch in a small room at the hospital with nothing to do. A nurse came in and asked if I'd like to see the baby. I don't remember seeing him, but I do remember visiting Mommy. There were people everywhere. My mother lay on a cot in the hall waiting for a room to open. She was smiling and looked very tired. Michael was born on November 15, 1955, at Tripler Hospital. Daddy and I walked out to the car holding hands.

Adjusting to a new baby was not easy. I had been an only child for eight years. I just found Daddy, who had been lost in Korea, and now I had to share him with a small baby who cried all the time.

Our Christmas tree was full of baby stuff. He needed a crib, a changing table, a swing, a playpen, and more gifts than I could count. There were always bottles in the sink and formula on the stove and diapers in the pail. This kid was a real nuisance.

On the other hand, he smiled when I held him and giggled when I tickled him.

Then, we prepared to move.

Baby Michael and Peggy

Given little notice and no choice, the military transferred First Lieutenant Albert V. Greene to Fort Devens in Massachusetts. We left Hawaii on a propeller-driven plane that landed in California. From there, Daddy drove us across the country, seeing family before reporting to our new post. I had the privilege of watching Michael in his bed carrier on the floor while I sat on the back seat. We stopped frequently and saw different landmarks across our country.

I learned the most important aspect of military dependent life: I became adept at making last-minute changes and accepting orders.

SIX

Adjustments

Fort Devens, Massachusetts (1956–1960)

With our visits to relatives complete, First Lieutenant Albert V. Greene and family reported for duty at Fort Devens in Massachusetts, just outside the little town of Ayer, which took about two hours of driving from Boston. Daddy worked as a company adjutant.

We lived in two different yet identical houses off base but within Devencrest military housing during our time at Fort Devens. The first stood on the east side of Devencrest, where lieutenants lived, and the second awaited on the west side for the time of my father's promotion to captain.

Army life, like a caste system, was segregated into officer and enlisted status. Although children of every ethnicity and from parents of every rank attended the same school, officers' families and enlisted personnel's dependents had separate swimming pools, recreation centers, clubs, and housing areas.

We children were called *army brats*. I thought all children of military personnel were given the name army brat, just like the Women's Army Corps were called WACs and soldiers GIs. I found out later that, at first, only officers' children were technically brats. But the word trickled down to encompass all of us—regardless of rank. We wore this label with pride.

The word *brat* never bothered me, so I didn't understand fully why my mother got mad at me when I called my brother a brat. Of course, I meant it derogatorily. Sibling rivalry was a natural and a maddening fact of life that transcended any caste system.

Michael was almost one year old when we moved to Devencrest. He cried a lot, and one day when I came home from school, he wasn't there. My mother and father had rushed him to the emergency room on the post, where, since the draft was still in effect, doctors and hospital staff were also soldiers. Only military personnel and their families had access to these facilities, which did not charge servicemen or their families.

I stayed with friends after school and listened to bits of neighborly concern. "It's such a shame. The baby's so little. He's sick, and no one knows what's wrong. Evelyn is so anxious."

My mother, always tired and worried, never smiled. I remember seeing her through the visitor's window rocking Michael. It seemed like forever while Mommy remained in the hospital caring for my brother.

I asked Daddy what was wrong. He said Michael was sick but would get better soon. I worried that he would die.

This was a difficult time in my life because, even though I loved the baby, I was jealous. I feared Michael's illness was my fault, and I felt guilty that he was so sick. I bargained with God. "Please, don't let my brother die," I prayed. "I don't really want him to go away. Please, make him better. If you do, I'll take care of him always."

I never learned what problem Michael had. Parents of the fifties thought children should be seen and not heard. They also believed keeping secrets from children would save them from worry. This meant I had no one I could talk to about my fears. We did not live close to any family like my grandparents.

Visits to medical facilities on base remained commonplace for my brother even after he came home. I often snuck into my parents' bedroom—after they moved his crib there—and placed my finger under his nose to reassure myself that he was still breathing. I decided my brother was important to me, and I became his protector even though petty arguments and sibling rivalry did land me in trouble. As we grew older, I still insisted on calling him The Brat.

Instead of learning to walk, Michael simply ran. His energy knew no bounds. My brother ran through the room, climbed the couch, leaped over it, and then bounced off the wall before running back through the room again. Whenever he sat, his legs straddled behind him as if he were ready to hop up and take off.

Hyperactivity was not recognized as a medical term in the late fifties and early sixties. Doctors thought so-called bad blood was the culprit. Now, looking back on this experience in my childhood, I am pleased that medical science has evolved out of the Dark Ages and discovered that chemical imbalances and the lack of oxygen during the early development of our nervous systems can cause hyperactivity in children. Today, I think much of Michael's lack of impulse control during his childhood may have resulted from his early illness.

I later saw many of the same symptoms Michael developed in my son, Keith. I immediately recognized that his hyperactivity and subsequent learning disabilities were because—like Michael—Keith was a sick baby. Unlike for Michael, procedures and strategies had become available for my son and other children like him and my brother.

Meanwhile, we all accepted the fact that Michael was all boy and could not be controlled or helped. I also decided he was simply a spoiled brat.

Every Saturday and on weekday evenings, Michael and I enjoyed watching *The Lone Ranger*, *The Cisco Kid*, *Have Gun Will Travel*, and *Bonanza* on our black-and-white television set with rabbit ears.

Cowboy movies were blockbusters. Neighborhood kids played cowboys and Indians and ran all over our backyard and the playground behind our house. Once, some boys made a noose and tried to hang some little kid in the tree. Fortunately, his mother found them and stopped it.

Our living quarters usually came with feline pets. When the army transferred folks, their pets were not included, and families often left their cats behind. We always seemed to inherit a cat or two that inevitably brought kittens.

"Mom!" I yelled one day while standing beside the door as I let the cat in. My brother must have been two or three at this time, for I had already attended the fourth grade. "Come get Michael. He's running like a wild Indian."

Zoom.

Michael ran past me, careening toward the door where we kept the box of kittens. He wore his cowboy hat and six-shooters, and he flew zapping through the house, over chairs and couches, and right into the box where the mama cat left her kittens. I screamed and pulled him out of that box, but it was too late.

My mother rushed to stand beside us. Mama Kitty skittered away. Michael and I looked into the box and watched as blood spurted from the ear of a little black kitty on which he fell. "Gee," Michael said. "He dies just like a cowboy."

Mommy sat with me at the kitchen table while I drank my cocoa and waited for the bus that took me to Fort Devens Elementary School on post. Most of the schools I attended were Department of Defense schools administered by our federal government rather than the public school system. These excellent DOD schools specialized in helping military families and children while exacting high standards.

My fourth-grade teacher's name was Mrs. Hall. I don't remember much about her, but I think I liked her and began to enjoy school. Report card subjects were reading and literature, English, spelling, penmanship, arithmetic, geography, history, science, music, and drawing. My report card indicated that my conduct was good or excellent. I was reading and writing well, but my math was only passable. Grades were given as numbers: one meant excellent, two was good, three meant fair or passable, four was unsatisfactory, and five was very poor. My favorite subjects must have been reading and writing because I consistently received twos on the card. I still wore glasses, but I do not remember being teased about them.

Mrs. Freemount, my fifth-grade teacher, was the worst teacher I have ever met. Her husband often brought their baby in a stroller and talked to her while she was supposed to be teaching. The work she assigned was too hard. I kept failing my spelling tests, and math was impossible. We talked in class, threw spitballs, and generally learned nothing. Mrs. Freemount didn't like me and often made me feel like a caged lion waiting for my trainer's whiplash. Recess was the only bright spot of the entire day, but one recess pushed me over the edge.

My girlfriend and I played pretend stories as we made them up in our secret spot behind a column on the far side of our school's field. Engrossed in our play, we failed to hear the school bell sounding the end of recess.

"Come on, Peggy!" my friend yelled as she ran like the wind, but the field fell silent before I noticed that everyone quietly waited, lined up at the front door.

"Margaret Greene," Mrs. Freemount boomed. "We had to wait several minutes for you to decide to join us. Because you are the reason we will lose our recess time tomorrow, you will stand here so everyone can look at you as they enter the class. You must take the blame. When the last child leaves, then you may come back to your seat."

The boys moaned, and the girls sneered, for they all knew it was my fault we would not have playtime the next day. I felt outcast and humiliated.

I hated that teacher.

The grading scale for fifth grade stated that E indicated superior work, G was good or above average, F was average work, U indicated unsatisfactory work, and VP, the worst, was very poor work.

On another occasion, Mrs. Freemount returned our math exams. Waving the papers into the air, she called our names and announced our grades.

"Margaret Greene. VP for arithmetic and VP for effort."

Then, she told us to take the papers home, have our parents sign them, and correct them. "If you do not bring them back corrected and signed, you will receive a VP. If you don't correct them, don't bother bringing them back."

Great, I thought, *just what I need, another VP—a triple VP. I don't know how to solve these problems. What am I going to do? I just won't bring the paper back. That way, I'll only have two VPs.*

The next day, Mrs. Freemount demanded, "Margaret Greene, where is your paper?"

"At home," I replied.

"Fine. Another VP. That gives you three VPs," she announced.

"No. You said we should not bring it back if we couldn't correct it. I—"

"Don't speak to me like that, young lady."

I burst out of the classroom and dashed into the hall as a torrent of tears streamed down my face. Somehow, I managed to get into the girls' restroom, where I stayed for a while. *This is not fair.*

Eventually, the principal and I had a quiet conversation. I believe someone called my mother. The principal told me to return to the lunchroom to join my already eating class. When I walked into the cafeteria, my classmates clapped! I sat next to my friend, who whispered, "Gee, you got guts."

After that, Mrs. Freemount pretty much ignored me until the last day of school. Mr. Ruppert, my father's friend and the director of the Army Band, arranged to have the band play a concert at my school for the final day's celebrations.

My classmates and I stayed in our room after the festivities to get our report cards directly from the teacher. Mrs. Freemount waited until the last moment to give me my report card. "Margaret Greene," she said, "I decided I couldn't fail you because the band came today."

Mrs. Freemont could not have failed me. My grades indicated average work across the board. Nevertheless, I owe a lot to Mrs. Freemount. She was the one teacher I never wanted to emulate in my teaching.

I did much better in sixth grade. Mrs. Carol Sakol taught using the same grading scale as in fifth grade. I managed good or above average to superior grades in every subject except arithmetic—which vacillated between good and average and back to good. During this year, I decided I wanted to become a teacher.

Even though spelling was one of my most difficult subjects, I won my sixth-grade class contest and had to participate in the school's grand spell-off at the end of the school year in 1959. A sea of eager faces looked at me from the auditorium floor while I stood—wearing my favorite blue skirt and white button-in-the-front blouse with its lace collar—on the stage beside six other contestants. After the first two rounds and eliminations, I remained standing with three others.

"The word is *lieutenant*."

The room hushed. I looked at my classmates, who waited with eyes wide. My fingers brushed the palms of my hands, and I closed my eyes. "Lieutenant," I said aloud. "L-I-E-T...E-T."

"No. I'm sorry. Please sit."

No? I thought. *Good. I can sit now.*

My classmates were more disappointed than I. My teacher hugged me and said, "Your father is a lieutenant, but that is a hard word to spell."

When I got home from school, I told my mother I lost the contest. She gave me a piece of cake. When Daddy entered the door, I ran to him and blurted that I had lost on the word *lieutenant*. I told him what my teacher said.

Daddy hugged me, smiled, and said, "It'll be easier from now on. Tell your teacher your father is a C-A-P-T-A-I-N now." He had been promoted from first lieutenant to captain, and he became the commanding officer of headquarters detachment that day. We celebrated with more cake, and then Mommy and Daddy went to a party at the Officers Club.

Despite having children to play with, making friends seemed difficult even though it was not unusual to play with somebody at one post, become separated by relocation, and then meet again at another. That's what happened with Donna. We were ten years old and in the fourth grade together.

Donna lived across the street from us in Massachusetts. I don't know if her father and mine had served together in another post, but our families were friends. Donna and I played jump rope, Hula-Hoop, and dolls. My mother often drank coffee with Donna's mother, which meant I had to play with Donna although we didn't get along very well.

I don't recall what happened, but I was blamed for something Donna did. This caused a tumultuous commotion at our house between my mother and me, so I ran away.

I was not running away to a foreign land, but rather I was running toward my father. I knew Daddy's company was on post—somewhere—so I walked from Devencrest toward the gate and past the guards. I cried, knowing I would get into more trouble when I got home, but I felt unfairly treated. I didn't know what to do or how to fix the situation, but I knew one thing: I was not going to take the blame for something I did not do.

Maybe Mr. Ruppert will help convince Daddy and Mommy not to get too mad at me. I wasn't sure where the Army Band or my father's office was, but I reasoned that I'd hear the band playing somewhere and just drop in.

Mr. Ruppert, Mommy and Peggy playing the piano
with Mommy looking on

"Little girl, are you all right?" a lady asked from her open car window.

I looked at the vehicle driving beside me on the road and ignored it.

"Are you lost?" the lady continued.

"No, I'm running away."

The car stopped, and a woman got out. She walked beside me. "Honey, come get in the car. We'll take you home. You shouldn't be walking alone here."

The two ladies from the car sat with me on the curb and listened to me cry. They convinced me to let them take me home and talk to Mommy. When we arrived at the house, Donna's mother was still there with my mother, and Mommy was crying.

"How dare you run away and scare your mother like that!" Donna's mother screamed.

Mommy brushed her aside and hugged me.

That was the last time I ran away.

Five years later, we met up with Donna again in Heilbronn, Germany. I refused to be her friend.

Either I outgrew the tendency to run away when things over-whelmed me, or I substituted this coping mechanism with another. About this time, I started fainting. I walked across a room, felt weak, got dizzy, and passed out. Down to the floor—I fell.

My family told me that sometimes I shook—but not all the time. At first, fainting was a scary thing that happened once in a while. As I grew older, I recognized when I was about to faint. My skin grew cold, and I felt like I was flying far away. At times, I saw colored lights. If I caught this feeling early enough, I found a place to lie on the floor and waited for the sensations to go away.

Sometimes, I fainted during a verbal fight with my mother, but mostly, I just fainted. Once, when I was in the fifth or sixth grade, I fainted suddenly. Mother told me I was shaking as if having a seizure. She called an ambulance that came to our house and took us all the way to a hospital in Boston.

There, the doctor attached a lot of electrodes to my scalp, flicked some switches, and watched a machine. Then, I waited outside while he talked with my mother. I don't recall being told why I fainted, but I believed I had epilepsy.

Losing my balance, feeling dizzy, and blacking out became a common thing for me. My thoughts never left me. I didn't know I had fallen or passed out because I had wonderful dreams of flying— until I woke with a jolt and screamed. I never hurt myself. Fainting didn't bother me as much as it did the people around me, so whenever this faraway feeling came upon me, I'd hide in the bathroom or in a corner until the feeling left or I lost consciousness.

At this point in my life, the vertigo became a welcome friend.

I thought everybody fainted. I also dropped things. I'd have a pencil in my hand—and then I didn't. I tripped over rocks and tree branches. *But doesn't everybody?* I'd joke with my playmates and say, "I have dropsy."

Seasons in Massachusetts changed. Autumn leaves turned many shades of green, red, purple, orange, and yellow before falling onto the ground, ready for raking in huge piles for jumping. Apples, cherries, and pumpkins added colors and scents to crisp winds that blew leaves over lawns for Halloween.

Winter snow allowed Daddy, Michael, and me to create snowmen, snow women, and snow rabbits. We also went on post to ice skate and toboggan. I especially enjoyed helping the neighbor boys build snow forts and having snowball fights. I loved the snow and used to pick Michael up and dangle him over the porch. I threw him into a snow pile. He'd sink into the fluff and giggle. Spring and summer were free and warm, but autumn and winter were best. By this time, Michael was about four, and I was twelve.

My friend Rosemary lived across the street from our home, so we attended seventh grade and the same Girl Scout troop together. Rosemary and I played and climbed trees in the playground behind her house. Close to our housing development, we roamed the wooded area and collected pine cones that we decorated with glitter. Then, Rosemary's father was transferred, and once again, I lost a friend.

Several weeks after Rosemary left, Maria and her brothers moved next door. Maria's father had been a prisoner of war in Korea and had his fingernails pulled out. That was gross. His hands looked like everyone else's—except the tips were calloused where nails should have been. Maria and I played with our paper dolls or Barbie dolls in the front yard—away from her brothers who played in the back.

A family from Puerto Rico lived next door to Maria. They spoke Spanish, so I didn't understand much of what they said. There were a little girl and boy about Michael's age. Two of the older boys were in the fourth and fifth grades. They had reputations for fighting.

Michael, five at this time, followed me around. One day, I noticed a commotion at the side of Maria's house and saw Michael standing beside her porch. There was much yelling and screaming directed toward Michael, but I couldn't understand anything said. The mother slammed her porch door and took after the group, screaming something.

Thinking Michael was in trouble and needed rescue, I ran toward the fray and screamed louder. I even hit one of the boys I thought was threatening my brother. Maria's mother also heard the commotion and interfered. She quickly sent Michael and me home while calming the situation. I still don't understand exactly what happened.

And yes, I got in trouble for that.

Every post was a self-contained community, divided from the civilian population by fences and a guarded gate. Each of us dependents wore our own army-issue dog tags and carried our own identification cards for entrance into the post exchange, commissary, movie theater, and other spots. The chapels on post opened to anyone who could enter the post gates. The chaplains, also soldiers, handled Protestant, Jewish, and Catholic services in the same building or, if available, in different chapels.

About this time in my life, I became religious. Daddy and I attended Catholic Mass every Sunday, but now I attended catechism twice every week after school too. A bus took all the Catholic boys and girls from our school to the church hall where nuns, wearing long black gowns and black scarves with white cardboard rims on their heads, taught us the text. Although my conduct in school was excellent, I tended to talk too much here. Punishment for talking out of turn meant I knelt straight on a prayer bench until the sister said I could return to my seat. This, of course, gave me something to confess every Saturday.

Not too long into the year, I was transferred upstairs to Sister Marion's class. She told us stories about the Nazi persecutions in Europe and how she and others tried to help the Jews. We did not read the Bible; we read a book called *The Catechism*, but Sister Marion's face lit up whenever she told the stories about Jesus and the saints. As we learned about the life of Jesus, we concentrated on his sacrifice, pain, and death for our sins. I became convinced that only Catholics could go to heaven, and I worried about my mother.

"Mommy, why don't you go to church on Sunday?" I asked one day as we walked with Michael toward the commissary.

"I stay home with the baby."

"Sister says only Catholics can go to heaven," I responded.

"If you keep bothering me about religion, I'll make you a Protestant," my mother said.

That was the last time I bugged my mother about religion.

Once a week, Girl Scouts met on post, where we held ceremonies, cookouts, and dances. We hiked a lot and learned how to mark and read a trail. We did not camp or put up tents; most badges taught girls skills in homemaking, crafts, and deportment.

My father, my mother, and I often danced on Saturday evenings at the Officers Club, so

Girl Scout Peggy

I knew how to dance. Our Girl Scout troop sponsored a dance class, and I invited my friend, Lyle, who happened to be a boy.

My first date was for the sixth-grade end-of-the-year dance held in the gym of our school. Daddy was the chaperone, and Lyle was my date. I wore a white rabbit fur over my shoulders, a pair of hose, and pumps. I wore lipstick for the first time. I was growing up. Our home movies showed Lyle, dressed in his suit, opening the car door and helping me into the car. Then, he closed the door and looked quite confused. Finally, he opened the door again and slid in next to me. Daddy drove us to the dance and stayed to chaperone.

Our family had a washing machine but no dryer. I often helped my mother hang the laundry on the line to dry. Whenever I went outside, Michael also came. We had a leash for my little brother and chained him to the clothesline so that he wouldn't run off. When we went shopping, I had charge of Michael. I held onto his leash and ran along beside or after him.

I played the piano—but not well. I saved my allowance of twenty-five cents per week and any money I happened to come upon until Mommy decided I had enough cash to buy a piano. When I was in sixth grade, we drove to Fishkill and purchased an upright, blond-paneled piano from Montgomery Ward. I was proud to give her my twenty-five dollars. My mother placed the instrument on layaway, but that piano was mine—I'd saved up for it and bought it with my own money.

My piano lessons took place downtown in Ayer, Massachusetts, on the bottom floor of a store on the main street. I walked from school to lessons and then home alone through the town and all the way to Devencrest. I enjoyed that walk—except when it snowed. I covered my shoes with plastic wrap if I forgot my boots.

I did not play with great skill, but I liked playing for myself at home. I practiced, and at recitals I played "Bells Are Ringing" and "Crunchy Flakes." I didn't enjoy recitals, however, so I begged off on them often.

Back in 1960, schools were divided into three sections. Elementary was from first through sixth grades, junior high was seventh and eighth grades, and high school was from ninth through twelfth grades. At the completion of each division, students and parents attended a graduation ceremony.

I went to my first public school since first grade during my seventh and the beginning of eighth grades at Ayer Junior High School. We military brats fraternized with the civilian population. There were no problems because the civilian population depended upon the post for employment. In subsequent moves, this was not the case.

Mr. McKenna, my favorite teacher, taught history, science, penmanship, English, and reading. He was a good teacher who discussed things with us and made us each feel important. My report card showed I had Cs in math but As and Bs in all other subjects.

In my bedroom, I made a chalkboard the focal point. I set my dolls up around my bed and taught them while doing my homework. Often, I reviewed lessons I learned that day and mimicked how my teachers taught. I wanted to be a teacher just like Mr. McKenna.

During the time I was growing up and learning, women rarely continued their education past high school. Few careers were open to women other than secretarial work, nursing, and teaching. Most girls believed they would graduate from high school, get married, and raise a family. Few mothers worked outside the home. I didn't think much about my future other than knowing I was going to college and wanted to teach.

I don't remember much about eighth grade other than Daddy's transfer just before the end of the year. I missed graduation and all the planned festivities with my school friends. I did walk down the aisle with my eighth-grade class in Fort Benning, Georgia, but I didn't know anybody, so it was not meaningful to me.

That transfer marked the first of several disappointments in missing end-of-the-year parties, functions, and graduations.

Adjusting to fast moves, changes in plans, and altered schedules became the norm. I learned that the only thing certain was uncertainty. To avoid disappointment, I decided not to look forward to anything. *If it happens, it happens. If not, well…*

Planning for the future is still not something I do.

SEVEN

A Different Culture

Fort Benning, Georgia (1961)

few months before my eighth-grade graduation, in the late spring of 1961, the military transferred my father from Fort Devens, Massachusetts, to Fort Benning, Georgia, where he attended the Nuclear Weapon Employment Course at the United States Army Infantry School. We loaded our blue, four-door Ford station wagon and drove through New York, Pennsylvania, and Illinois visiting relatives. I sat in the back seat, irritated that I would not be graduating with my friends.

As we traveled from north to south, the weather became hot, muggy, and rainy. Towns appeared run-down, and agriculture dominated. Everywhere we looked, black people loitered. This was a different culture from what I had known.

I had heard about the civil rights movement, but it was not something that affected my life—until we moved to Georgia. When we stopped at a diner in Mississippi along the way, my understanding of racial issues changed.

Dad went into the diner. Michael, Mom, and I followed.

A few black people sat separated from others, who happened to be white. A sign over the counter read *Niggers not served*. In my experiences, black or brown people were called coloreds or Negroes but not that word.

We sat to eat, but after looking around the establishment, my father got up and stormed out, taking us with him. "If they can't eat, neither will we," he said.

Baffled and hungry, I asked why we couldn't eat there.

"Because I don't want to support a place so bigoted," Daddy said.

We had stumbled upon a sit-in where black Americans, in a peaceful demonstration for their equal rights under the Constitution, entered diners and other establishments that posted signs stating they would not be served. This confused me. Why was there a sign saying such things?

Daddy explained more. "You know that slavery ended after the Civil War. However, Jim Crow laws were passed allowing the separation between blacks and whites. Those laws are now not accepted."

"How come wherever we go, blacks and whites are together?"

"In 1954, all military services were desegregated. Sometimes there are problems, but blacks and whites use the same facilities. We're still hungry. Let's find a place to eat."

Although most army brats were white, I played with everyone and accepted all others without noticing their color, race, or religion. I didn't think of the Negro people as being any different from Caucasians or Orientals. Black soldiers marched just like the rest; their children played just like the rest. However, I would not meet an African-American officer until 1966.

While we lived in Georgia, Daddy met many officers from foreign countries that were allies of the United States. We became special friends with the Rapold family. Major Rapold, an official in the Swiss Army, had adopted a dark-skinned girl named Nathalie while stationed in India. Two smaller Rapolds had skin whiter than mine. Michael was the same age as the Rapold boy, so they played often. Nathalie and I became best friends.

Our families toured the Georgia countryside together. One Saturday, we drove to a public beach. We children jumped into the water ready for a day of fun, but Nathalie noticed that parents took their children out of the water and seemed to point at her. We continued playing until Mr. Rapold ordered us out of the lake.

We stood beside our mothers while Dad and Mr. Rapold talked with an official. The other swimmers returned to the water, but we could not.

"Come on," Daddy said. "Get in the car. We're not wanted here."

Later, my father explained that after Mr. Rapold told the official Nathalie was really from India, the official stated that we could swim, but he also said, "This beach is for whites only. The niggers have one of their own."

Neither Mr. Rapold nor Dad wanted to stay in such a prejudiced place. Nathalie picked up her towel and walked silently to the car. I felt confused, then angry. *How can people be so cruel? All we want to do is swim.*

Later that same day, we stopped at a shack with a gas pump for fueling cars. Nathalie and I rode together, and we got out of the car to get a drink from the water fountain. There were two.

One fountain bore a sign that read *colored*. The other showed no label.

"What color do you suppose this water is?" Nathalie asked.

"I don't know. Let's try it and see."

Both fountains spouted the same color water. We felt disappointed.

After arriving at our new post, we stayed in several rooms in the VOQ, the visiting officers quarters, while we waited for a duplex in the housing area. Michael went to kindergarten, and I started school at the tail end of eighth grade. I was the new girl in this DOD school on post, but the kids accepted me easily. We had all been new at some point.

Although all girls took home economics, by the time I entered the class, the sewing machines were either taken or broken, so I had little to do but sit.

The teacher of English literature, however, assigned my group— two boys and me—to read and create a play that presented the true meaning of the poem "Oh Captain! My Captain!" by Walt Whitman. I researched the poem and wrote an essay on its interpretation, but the boys wanted to create a spoof. I read the poem in class while the boys acted out some ridiculous yet hilarious scenes.

The class laughed. So did the teacher. "That was interesting and humorous," she said. "But it is not the true meaning of the poem." We got a C.

I was not happy.

Before my family arrived in Georgia, I had not studied a foreign language, so when the school told me I had to learn enough French to pass a test to graduate from eighth grade, I panicked.

Fortunately, the teacher explained that all she would expect me to know was the current unit. They were learning about setting a table and ordering a meal in French. Not having heard the language, I felt lost, but I took the book home every night.

I studied diligently under a bright light at a desk in a dark corner of the VOQ and memorized: *des converts, un couteau, une fourchette, une cuilliere, une assiestte, une tase, un plat, une table, une serviette. Merci beaucoup.* My favorite word—*une serviette*, the only French I retained—meant one napkin. If I ever went to France, I'd be able to ask for one napkin.

In science class, the students were studying the biology of insects, another topic I had not encountered. I learned to copy a diagram from the board and correctly label the parts of a grasshopper on that diagram. The grasshopper had a thorax—a fact I long remembered. The skill of diagramming lasted longer; it would come in handy during my biology classes in high school and college.

On Friday, May 5, 1961, right after I arrived in school, a bell rang. I thought we were having a fire drill. Instead, the student body marched onto the grass field around our school and looked up into the sky. We waited and waited in an orderly fashion like good soldiers until we heard the announcement: Alan Shepard had blasted off in the *Mercury* spacecraft.

I saw a line streak upward in the distance.

We clapped and gave each other hits on the back in congratulations. Luckily, the teachers gave permission for us to sit. About fifteen minutes later, another streak appeared from above falling toward the earth. After sitting in the Georgia heat, we felt eager to return to our air-conditioned classrooms.

A month later, Michael and I graduated on the same day. In the morning, five-year-old Michael wore a white dress shirt, dark suit pants, and a jacket with a white handkerchief in the pocket. Daddy tied a tiny, dark tie around his neck. Michael walked solemnly down the school corridor with other kindergarten kids and disappeared into the auditorium where Mom and Daddy waited with the other parents.

In the evening, I wore a simple, pastel-colored, princess-style dress; a pair of hose; and my new, white pumps. We wore white mortarboard graduation skullcaps. Feeling awkward and not knowing any of my classmates, I walked alone among a crowd of smiling kids. Some wore lovely corsages attached to their dresses.

I was about to enter high school—somewhere.

Just before summer vacation began, we moved from the VOQ into a duplex where service families lived while on temporary duty. Families moved in and out all the time.

One job that fell to me with each relocation was to inventory household equipment. Every time we moved, a listing was made of items packed for military-paid shipment of household goods. I made another list for storage—if we chose to store belongings at our own cost—as well as another for furnishings we borrowed from the housing department for temporary use. I didn't witness who did the packing—they, whoever they were, generally completed it during my day at school—but Mom and I did the unpacking.

As usual, whenever we moved into new quarters, my mother and I set about cleaning. She was a good housekeeper who always kept our homes clean, neat, and tidy. I learned how to wash window blinds in the bathtub and how to wash, dry, and put dishes away without access to a dishwasher. We owned a vacuum cleaner, but I dusted, swept, and mopped while Mom used the vacuum. I most detested the job of cleaning the bathroom—especially scrubbing the tile floor, toilet, and tub. Every time we left army quarters, we cleaned again to pass the inspection required before signing our residence back to the service.

"Mom," I asked, "why do we have to clean this already cleaned house?"

"You don't want to live in someone else's dirt, do you?" Then, ignoring my assertion that the house wasn't dirty, she added her catchall phrase: "Because I said so."

My mother did not permit me to do laundry in the washing machine, but I had the job of hanging it out on the line to dry and retrieving it in the evening. Permanent press had not been invented yet, so all clothing needed ironing. Mom hired a black maid named Daisy to do that job, and she taught me to iron—a chore I enjoy to this day.

Daisy and I often talked while we ironed. Her children attended an all-black school in town. She told me it was crowded and not as good as the other school, but "tha's the way it's always been. They's nothin' we can do 'bout it." She wished her kids could get a better education. Daisy didn't like having to sit in the back of the bus, but she said, "I knows my place and don't make no trouble."

My early friendships with other military children and conversations like those I had with Daisy led me to believe all people should have the same rights as everyone else.

In 1969, just seven years after the disturbing, prejudicial encounters my family and I experienced when we moved to the South, I would volunteer as the first student teacher from Northwestern State College integrated into an all-black school in Shreveport, Louisiana. I would also agree, five years later, to teach in a segregated, black, inner-city school in Houston, Texas, and again in Dade County, Florida, in 1989. It seemed strange to me that true integration had not been achieved in the schools in which I taught. However, state systems often fell far behind national government's laws by integrating teachers rather than students. The tendency of the white population to leave the public system left those public schools with a predominantly minority population.

Rapid changes occurred during the sixties. Shootings, bombings, and lynchings fueled hatred between the races. People tripped on illegal drugs such as heroin and LSD. Even civilian schools faced issues with drugs like marijuana. General unrest brought about by court-ordered integration via busing led to a call for change.

Conflicts arose between communism, democracy, dictatorship, and capitalism.

Elvis was king, but our country elected a young, handsome, dynamic man with a beautiful, fashionable wife as our president. By the time Daddy graduated from the Nuclear Weapons Employment Course, Kennedy had been president for a few months.

Like many baby boomers, I admired President Kennedy when in 1961 he said, "Ask not what your country can do for you. Ask what you can do for your country." He initiated fitness requirements for students and the Peace Corps program. He took responsibility for the Bay of Pigs disaster and pressured the Russians into removing their missiles from Cuba.

The Cold War heated up with the Union of Soviet Socialist Republics—better known as Russia—and Red China as our enemies. Rockets blasted off carrying capsules containing astronauts into space. A race to land a human on the moon ran between the USSR and the USA. The fear of radiation from an atomic blast caused panic. People prepared for nuclear annihilation.

In August 1961, President Kennedy built up our armed forces while the Russians built the Berlin Wall. Orders arrived for Daddy's departure to Germany on an unaccompanied tour.

The family decided to drive from Fort Benning, visit relatives in the Northeast, and look for a place in Mom's hometown of Peekskill, New York. Our family would stay there while Daddy went away—again. Although I felt ready to exchange the heat of Georgia for the cooler climate up north, once more, like a dandelion, I was blown to a new location where I needed to grow new roots. This time, however, the roots had previously been planted.

Troubles

New York (1961)

I don't remember many details about the trip from Georgia back to New York, but our family must have driven the car, our preferred mode of transportation. Along the way, we visited reconstructed Georgia plantations, toured past slave quarters, and watched a local dredging operation attempt to rescue a sunken Confederate ship.

We also drove into Washington, DC, and stopped at important sites. I walked up the steps of the Lincoln Memorial, and I saw the original Constitution of the United States in a glass case. Either there were demonstrations in the nation's capital, or we were short on time. We didn't stay long enough for more sightseeing.

After my family and I visited with relatives, we shopped for houses in Mahopac, New York, which was close to Peekskill. Usually, a home waited for us in the military housing area, but this time, we had to find a place within the civilian town. I still remember Daddy's one request of the real estate agent: We must have a house with an existing bomb shelter.

My parents considered three or four homes with areas that could serve as shelters in a nuclear disaster. As I walked into those small spaces—usually under or at least at the same level as a basement—I wondered. *How on earth could this little place protect anyone from atomic radiation?* In the end, my mother and father chose for us to stay in an apartment in Peekskill close to Grandma Mabel's house.

Mom and Daddy slept on a couch in the living room. Michael and I slept in separate beds in the bedroom. The house held one bathroom and a kitchen. The living room also served as a dining area. Although my parents never discussed their plans with me, I believed we would remain in this apartment for a short time—until Daddy would send for us to join him in Germany.

In the meantime, Daddy wanted Michael to attend St. Mary's Parochial School to receive a Catholic education. The nuns, however, refused to accept my brother because our mother was not Catholic. At least, that's what happened at first. Daddy then donned his uniform, walked my brother down to the school and into the office, and explained that he had been called away in the service of his country and therefore had to leave his family.

The nuns accepted Michael, and Daddy went away.

Michael, only six years old and still very active, behaved a bit out of control. Our mother had her hands full with a hyper little boy and a headstrong teenager. I resented having to watch The Brat, so Mom and I argued often.

My little brother didn't like school—or the very strict nuns. For homework, he had to write "$1 + 1 = 2$" twenty times in his composition book and repeat this exercise for each simple addition equation. I questioned how anyone could teach a young kid how to add this way, especially a small boy who couldn't sit still for three seconds.

Like I'd done when I was younger, my brother ran away from school. Mom called my grandmother and my uncles to look for Michael, but no one could find him. I set out as soon as I arrived home from school, but when I reached downstairs, Michael walked up toward me through the parking lot on his way home. A taxi driver had seen him wandering around town and driven him to our house.

Unlike me after running away, Michael got in no trouble.

The civilian high school I attended, larger than any DOD school I had known, started us out in the auditorium for homeroom. Every ninth-grader sat and waited until the bell rang before we separated for our classes. My schedule included geography, German, algebra, physical education, and English.

My geography teacher happened to live in our apartment complex. I had a crush on him. I tried to miss the bus after school as often as possible, and he drove me home until near Halloween. He told me his wife didn't want him to give me a ride anymore, so I would need to call a taxi, and I accepted that. After all, he was a married man!

One day, this geography teacher ran late for our class. A fistfight erupted between two boys. My teacher rushed into the room, dumped his briefcase on the floor, and pulled the boys apart. Then, he hit one of the boys in the chest.

Shocked, I wondered why the teacher did such a thing.

My favorite teacher left class and didn't return for several days. When he resumed teaching, the two boys were already gone.

As military dependents, we all knew that any misbehavior in a DOD school reflected upon our fathers' military records. Although rare disturbances occurred, the office took care of them by immediately notifying each offender's father's commander. Infractions were few. Not so in a civilian school.

Another change I noted in this school—compared to those I had attended previously—hinged on the importance placed upon who our fathers were and what they did. When my classmates asked what my father did, I proudly stated that he was a soldier in Germany.

The boys heckled me. "Your dad is a killer. Killer."

A killer? I thought. I had never considered that. I knew he trained with a gun and had fought in wars, but a killer? These boys' accusations stayed with me until I had a chance to speak with my father about this later—after we had settled in Germany. He told me that, yes, he had killed people during wartime in defense of himself, his buddies, and his country. "I'm a defender," he said.

Meanwhile, high school algebra completely confused me. *How on earth can anyone add, subtract, multiply, or divide letters? Why do I have to learn this?*

I had missed several weeks at the beginning of school, and I stayed only for the first grading period. In that time, I made one friend. Her name was Kathy.

Kathy and I took gym together and rode the same bus home. We spent afternoons at her house talking and cutting out pictures from magazines. She introduced me to her friend Mary, who lived down the street from my grandmother in Roe Park. After I moved away, Kathy and I kept in contact through letters throughout my high school years. We met again before I started college at Alfred University in 1965. But tragedy would strike when Kathy died in an automobile accident in 1966, just one week before she was to visit me at college.

I still had fainting spells during school—at least once a week. My heart beat quickly, my eyesight blurred, I perspired, and then I felt far away. I didn't tell anyone about these fleeting feelings. Whenever I sensed one coming on, I walked close to the wall, touching it until the dizziness left. In hindsight, these were probably anxiety attacks.

Daddy had been away for two months. Things had not been good without him, but they were about to get worse.

When not in school, I spent as much time as possible in front of the television, dancing to *American Bandstand*. Michael spent his time running, jumping, and making a racket.

Shortly before Thanksgiving, Grandma and Grandpa Greene visited. Grandpa presented Michael with a toy gun he had renovated. It made noise and glowed with a red light when he pulled the trigger. Grandpa Patrick was very proud of his invention, but Michael showed no interest and threw a big fit. Grandpa said it was all right, but our mother, upset, disagreed. That evening, Grandma and Grandpa Greene returned to Greenpoint.

Because Mom was hosting the family for Thanksgiving dinner, she drove my brother and me to the commissary at West Point for groceries. On the way over Bear Mountain, someone hit the back of our car. The impact threw Michael across the back seat. No one was injured, and insurance paid for the car, but the incident shook up everyone.

Two days later, Grandma Purdy stopped by. She wanted to help plan the family gathering for Thanksgiving, but there was a problem with the turkey. When I arrived home from school that day, Grandma discussed something with my mother and then left—angry.

At that point, Michael ran through the room hollering, and he threw something at me.

I took off after him. I yelled, "Mom, come get this brat!"

My mother fell.

She lay unconscious.

I called Grandma Purdy, who contacted her doctor and the rest of the family.

After Dr. Moody placed Mom in my bed, he pronounced that she had suffered a nervous breakdown.

We needed to contact my father.

That evening, my mother's brother, my uncle Richie, came to the apartment and insisted that he read my father's letters. He was certain Daddy had said something to Mom to cause her breakdown.

I refused to give him the letters. He looked through the drawers of our desk and Mom's dresser. All the while, I sat fuming. When he found them, he read them and said, "There's nothing in these that would cause Evelyn any problem."

"How dare you read private mail!" I screamed. "It's none of your business what my parents write to each other."

Uncle Richie jumped up from his seat and left.

When I calmed down, I realized I should not have spoken so harshly to an adult, even though I knew I was right. Thanksgiving was around the corner. I needed to apologize. I called his house and spoke with my cousin.

"Kathy," I said, "I need to speak with your dad."

"Peggy, he's so mad at you. He won't even let Patty or me speak to you." She hung up.

Rather than being angry or sad, I wondered how an adult could act like such a child. I was not permitted to speak with or see my cousins.

Nevertheless, Uncle Richie contacted the Red Cross, which called Daddy in Germany.

We waited several days that seemed like weeks before my father walked in the door. As soon as he entered the bedroom, my mother opened her eyes, smiled, and sat up.

Within a week, Mom, Michael, and I had tickets on a civilian airline for Frankfurt, Germany.

My mother, my brother, and I arrived at Frankfurt in Germany only minutes before Daddy's military flight on December 10, 1961. My father's mother, Grandma Margaret, had mentioned earlier that her mother left Germany years before on that date.

From there, we took a train to Heilbronn. Since Daddy's orders still stated that this was an unaccompanied tour, we paid our own transportation and found an apartment in town. According to military jargon, we were *on the economy*.

Cold War

Heilbronn, Germany (1961–1962)

At first, the Cold War did not seem a reality to me. I heard it referred to on the news, but its effect on me was merely academic. Kids talked about *the Red Menace*, meaning the USSR, and how President Khrushchev might get mad and push a button sending missiles our way. After all, he had yelled a lot and banged his shoes on a table at a United Nations meeting in 1960. What would a man who could do that be capable of if he got angry? The adults around me feared nuclear war. News and magazine commentaries described the USSR's—Russia's—way of life as that of an enemy. The two governments—democratic and communist— were pitted against each other. What would happen if this war occurred and freedom lost?

I learned that the United States had been the only country with atomic weaponry prior to 1950, but other nations, especially the Soviet Union, quickly developed such capabilities. When I saw student renditions of family bomb shelters at the school's science fair, I shook my head and thought it was only a fear tactic. All this changed when Dad transferred to Germany during the building of the Berlin Wall.

We moved into the upstairs apartment of a building managed by a woman from East Berlin. Fraulein Schmidt escaped communist rule several years earlier and worked at the Wharton Barracks or *Kaserne* post exchange. She later became friends with us when my parents decided to wallpaper our apartment, in this way increasing the value of her property.

The day after we arrived at Heilbronn, however, Dad left for maneuvers.

Even though my mother had suffered what the doctor called a nervous breakdown, she managed to handle setting up house in a land where she didn't understand the language. I never learned how she managed to acquire food for us, cook, do the dishes, make sure we had hot water for our baths, wash the clothes, or clean house at that time.

Dad was away, and we had no transportation.

The apartment—furnished with beds, a table, six chairs, two dressers, a very long desk, and a sofa—needed items from the military lending closet. Within a week, linens, dishes, and a few pots and pans arrived. Getting a refrigerator took a little longer. The few items we had packed before leaving the United States waited in storage until Dad's orders changed from unaccompanied to accompanied status. When that time came a month later, the allotted shipment arrived.

To heat our apartment, we had to carry coal from the basement to the ground floor and up another flight of stairs and then finally make a fire with kindling. Our kitchen stove also used the dirty, black fuel and had one gas burner. On that stove, we heated cold water from the tap to augment our baths. Mom stored milk on the windowsill between the shutter and the glass window because we still had no refrigerator.

The apartment stayed cold. Our mother wore her fur coat as a bathrobe when she woke us for school, which we enrolled in just before Christmas. At first, Mike and I dressed under the covers. The school bus picked us up on the corner across from our house. Mike attended first grade, and I was in ninth grade at the DOD school serving military personnel in Heilbronn, which taught kindergarteners through freshmen.

Dad returned from maneuvers after about two weeks. He looked tired but smiled and got right down to seeing that we were "situated," as he called it. His assignment at that time was with Headquarters Company, 1st Armored Battalion, 54th Infantry, 4th Division. He was the *assistant battalion S3*, which, as I understood it, meant he helped with training soldiers in case they were to go to war. The possibility of war was always a consideration while we lived in Germany. This is when the Cold War became a reality to me.

More than 350 miles northeast of Heilbronn, the divided city of Berlin—in sectors run by the British, French, and Soviets—was 111 miles inside East Germany. Between 1949 and 1961, more than two million skilled workers fled into West Germany through Berlin, hoping to partake in the high standard of living in the west. To stop East German citizens from leaving, East German soldiers and militia surrounded West Berlin.

On August 13, 1961, only four months prior to our arrival, East Germans woke to barbed wire fencing. A temporary fortification closed access to the west and blocked the free flow to Berlin through East Germany. Quickly, a concrete wall manned with machine gunners and a mined no-man's-land appeared.

While we lived in Germany, *The Stars and Stripes* newspaper reported many escape attempts that ended in violence. Tensions mounted. I became more aware of international politics, especially as we drove across the countryside where tanks and troop trucks convoyed. The soldiers, not much older than I, waved.

I soon learned how the Berlin Wall impacted someone close to our family.

One day, after we'd lived in our Heilbronn apartment for a few months, Fraulein Schmidt asked to speak with my dad. He sent me out of the room during their conversation. I overheard enough to realize the tenseness of the political climate of the time. Fraulein Schmidt told my father that she had been allowed to leave East Germany because she spoke excellent English and could infiltrate US military posts to gather intelligence. She had been moving from place to place, hoping to avoid the Soviet Committee for State Security—the KGB. Meanwhile, her family in East Berlin had been threatened by the Stasi, the East German secret police, because she had not been sending any intelligence. She wanted my father to help her.

I don't know what, if anything, he did.

Fraulein Schmidt disappeared a few weeks later.

Although we still lived on the economy, day-to-day life grew easier for us after we bought a small, used Volkswagon. We made our first trip to the coal depot. Dad drove to show Mom the way. Once we'd purchased our coal, I was given the duty to be sure the coal bin was full every day. Walking up and down the stairs into that dark, cold, basement scared me, but after we fixed the light hanging on its string—so I could see without a flashlight—the basement wasn't so bad.

Then, wonders of wonders, our party-line telephone arrived. It was a black roller phone with a receiver. When the bell rang twice in succession, I answered, "Captain Greene residence. Peggy speaking." If a man responded, I was to say, "Yes, sir. One minute, sir," and fetch my father. If a woman, I said, "Yes, ma'am," and gave the phone to my mother. If a friend called, I asked parental permission to speak but then stayed on the line for three minutes. I set the egg timer beside the phone. To my relief, these rules relaxed some after we moved into housing on post.

After my parents bought the car, Mom sometimes picked us up after school, and we went to the commissary, post exchange, or snack bar on post to eat. When Dad returned from training, he worked in an office at headquarters and met us at the Officers Club for dinner before taking us home.

I noticed that the Germans hung only white lights for Christmas. Back in the States, one of our family traditions included decorating with colored lights. We strung one multihued light strand around each of our windows in town. Mike and I also cut paper chains and hung them inside.

Every year, our family placed a star on top of our tree and filled the branches with ball ornaments, decorations we made, and candy canes. We ate one each night for seven days after Christmas. I don't remember a "Greene" Christmas tree in 1961, but I do remember that the family downstairs decorated their beautiful live Christmas tree with candles, which they lit only for dinner when the family was at home or when company arrived.

Our candy canes that year stood on the dinner table in a boot-shaped container.

While we lived in Germany, we adopted some local customs and incorporated them into our family traditions. On December 6, German children placed shoes outside their doors, and an elf came by in the night to leave sticks or candy in each shoe, depending upon its owner's behavior. Since we missed this tradition—by half a week—Dad suggested we do it a few nights before Christmas. He assured us the elves would arrive.

In the morning, Mike ran out the door, found his shoe, ran back in, and flailed his sticks through the air. "Look—I got swords."

My brother and I received both candy and sticks, indicating we were sometimes good and sometimes bad. This confused me. I thought my brother deserved only sticks. Although I loved him and was very protective of him, he and I fought often.

At the time of our childhood, few understood ADHD, attention deficit hyperactivity disorder, a possibly inherited mental condition nowadays controlled with behavior modification and certain medications. Military doctors simply told us Mike's impulsive, highly active behavior showed he was "all boy."

I remember one incident in particular while we lived in Heilbronn and Dad was away.

I had settled at the table with my homework while Mom and a friend sat on the sofa a room away. Mike dashed close to me, grabbed my almost completed homework from the table, giggled, and turned to run. "Michael, you better give that back!" I yelled.

"No," he spat.

I lunged toward him. The chair crashed to the floor as he darted away and out the door. "Mom, get Mike! Stop him," I demanded.

Mom did what she always did. She ignored the noise, so I had to take action myself.

I didn't want to hurt him, but the little twerp had something that belonged to me. I pursued my six-year-old brother as he jumped over beds and scurried under tables. All the while I chased him, I glanced at my mother, hoping she would intervene.

She didn't.

Enraged, I saw red. I pulled Mike onto the floor, placed my hands around his neck, and squeezed.

I saw my actions in slow motion as if on a television screen. The ringing in my ears seemed to place me in an eerie vacuum. No noise. Complete quiet. My brother was choking, and nobody was helping him.

My hands opened.

Mike leaped up and ran off.

I had become so furious that I tried to kill my own brother.

"Mom, how could you let me do this?" I cried. "I could have hurt him."

"But you didn't, Peggy," Mom said.

I tossed in bed at night, worried and ashamed of myself. How could I have gotten so angry? As a devout Catholic teenager who seriously studied mortal and venial sins, I had committed the mortal sin of attempted murder. I felt so ashamed of myself for trying to murder my brother that I went to church to discuss this with the priest.

I sat in the little side chapel, praying and gathering the courage to go to confession.

"Bless me, Father, for I have sinned."

"Yes, my child."

"Uh, um, I got so mad at my brother. I...I...um...tried to kill him." Tears streaked down my cheeks as I sobbed. "I was so angry! He took my paper and wouldn't give it back. My mother did nothing. I got really furious!"

"Calm down. Did you kill him?" the priest asked.

Shocked at his question, I blurted, "No. I put my hands around his neck and squeezed, but I let go, and he was okay. It's a mortal sin!"

"You did not commit a mortal sin. God forgives you. Please stay a few minutes so we can talk. For your penance, say three Hail Marys and one Our Father."

During that conversation after confession, the priest explained that sibling rivalry was normal. He told me it took courage to admit what I had done.

I needed to find better ways to deal with anger.

Herr and Frau Kuhn lived downstairs in our apartment house. Herr Kuhn reminded me of my Grandfather Patrick. Both were about the same age and had a full head of absolutely white hair. Each stood over six feet tall, straight, and proud. Grandfather Patrick had fought in the Great War, World War I. Herr Kuhn remembered that war but was too young to fight. He did fight for *the mother country* during the Second World War, but he insisted several times that he was not a Nazi.

Neither Herr Kuhn nor Frau Kuhn spoke English, so I tried my beginning German on them. They happily helped with my learning. Sometimes, they took me with them when they walked the hiking trail over the hill to the ancient ruins of a medieval castle called Götzenturm. That wasn't the only hiking I did in Heilbronn.

Wherever my family posted, I joined the Girl Scouts in an effort to make friends. In Germany, I was old enough to join the Senior Scouts. However, there were none, so I chose to help with the younger kids—a Brownie troop. The Brownies, giggly girls in first and second grades, ran and explored everywhere. There were so many of them—at least twenty per troop—their leaders and mother-volunteers needed teenage help to keep up with the children. I was it.

Fortunately, I knew basic first aid and how to mark and follow a trail, so the girls and I romped through the woods and over hills. Twice during our stay in Heilbronn, I took them hiking. We discovered insects, rocks, and moss on trees. Thankfully, we never tripped over any unexploded mines or found live ammunition during these excursions—although there were incidents reported nearby now and then.

One evening, Mike and I enjoyed a rare, relatively quiet time playing pick-up sticks on the sofa when Dad entered the apartment. He tossed his cap onto the table and announced, "You'll never believe who I saw today."

Mom left the kitchen, entered our room, and sat beside Mike while we all waited for Dad to tell his story.

"I was sitting at my desk working on the usual paperwork," Dad said. "I didn't pay any attention to the noises around me, but then I heard a familiar, metallic sound like *click...clack...click*. Something inside of me froze." Dad waited, letting the suspense build.

"I was signing the day's report, but my pen just stopped. I lifted my head and saw a big German standing before me. I did not recognize the man immediately." Dad bent over the coffee table and slid his finger along it before continuing.

"Then, he wiped his gloved finger across the top of my desk—and I stood at attention."

Dad looked up at our blank faces and explained. "It was Max, one of the German soldiers who guarded me in the prison camp in Italy during the war." Max had worn white gloves in the camp and had run his finger over surfaces to check for dust.

I had never before heard Dad say anything about his experiences as a soldier during the Second World War. I knew he had been a prisoner of war but nothing more of his World War II stories.

Although Max served as a guard during Dad's confinement, they developed a camaraderie. Max had an uncle who ran the fish shop on the corner in Brooklyn, where my father's family lived, and Max spoke excellent English. He had taken my father—with a gun pointed at his back—out of the compound several times. They had engaged in many conversations during that time.

Like my father, Max had stayed in his country's military after the war and was living in Heilbronn. I did not learn how Max knew Dad was there or whether it was a chance meeting, but Max and his wife joined Mom and Dad for the German-American Ball that weekend. Max gave me a postage stamp from the Nazi era, which is probably in the family stamp albums that were given to my brother. This experience with meeting Max and hearing my father's stories brought history to life and started my interest in my family's and others' life stories.

My own life story expanded as my freshman classes included German, algebra, physical science, English literature, world history, and gym. Dance was my elective.

Algebra made no sense to me. It confused me. Letters were for words, numbers for math. How could I be expected to add and subtract letters? Wasn't it like adding apples to bananas? Did $2a$ (apples) $+ 3b$ (bananas) $= 5x$ (fruit salad)?

I was so far behind. I would have given up completely if I had not had a crush on Mr. Boyd, my teacher who taught not just algebra but also gym and dance—and never raised his voice. Single and in his late twenties, he had a round, boyish, clean-shaven face with short, blond hair and blue eyes. Every day, he wore a different bow tie with his white, short-sleeved dress shirt. When he smiled, I melted. I asked questions, and he answered them, but on one occasion the assignment completely baffled me.

I couldn't understand his answer. After he tried to help me, he sent me back to my desk and started assisting another student.

Frustrated, I returned to my seat and slammed my books on the table, causing a tremendous *bang*.

The class quieted. All eyes focused on me. Not knowing what else to do, I grinned.

"Are you finished?" Mr. Boyd asked.

My face turned beet red. I wanted to hide. Instead, I sat down, folded my hands, and waited for the bell to ring.

On gym days, we girls changed into our white, short-sleeved shirts and blue shorts with spotless white sneakers before entering the gym where Mr. Boyd took attendance. Afterward, we lined up, returned to the locker room, and showered before changing into our school clothes. A girl was assigned to check that we each showered. I felt humiliated every time we did this. I had not yet developed like many of the other girls.

One day, each girl jumped on a trampoline in the gym. I didn't want to.

Mr. Boyd said, "You look scared. You can do it."

Then, he picked me up and threw me onto the trampoline.

I slapped him.

Mr. Boyd stepped back but said nothing.

All the girls groaned, and I jumped on the trampoline.

Mr. Boyd ignored me, but my stomach leaped higher than my feet. *I slapped a teacher. What am I going to do? How can I ever go to class again?*

That evening, I met Dad at the Officers Club. Mr. Boyd happened to be eating there as well.

I couldn't sit still. I started shaking.

Dad noticed something was wrong. After I told him what I had done, he told me not to worry but insisted I apologize to Mr. Boyd.

Mr. Boyd was gracious and smiled when I approached.

"I'm sorry I hit you," I stammered.

"That's okay," he said. "See you in class tomorrow." He was the first—and last—teacher I hit.

Growing up in the military was different from growing up in one place. Most children at this time stayed in the same town throughout their childhood, lived close to relatives, and attended school with their buddies. Many married their high school sweethearts. In several ways, military life was similar. The military became our family.

Every base or post contained the same buildings as civilian towns. Only the personnel changed. Because we were all in the service, often people crossed paths in different places. This happened several times for me.

Donna, the friend with whom I had a falling out four years before at Fort Devens in Massachusetts, appeared in my freshman class in Heilbronn. We didn't speak, but our parents had remained friends, so when our families visited, she and I walked downstairs to the parking lot where other kids congregated. There, we ignored each other.

It was always difficult for me to make friends. I made lots of acquaintances. It hurt too much when a friend left me or if I left that friend. Basically a shy person, I could put on a show in an effort to hide that shyness.

Joe, who stood only a few inches taller than I did, was smart and funny. He smiled easily and had one blue eye and one light-brown eye. We met at our lockers and walked to class together. During our elective, we learned to dance, and we attended sock hops after school. I smiled a lot. We were both fourteen.

My father's orders changed. Instead of being *S3*, he now became *S2* and worked mostly in the office at headquarters, which was directly across the street from the Officers Club and behind our school building. At the time, of course, he didn't tell any of us this. The S2 was responsible for security. He was transferred again just after school ended in June 1962.

Dad drove us to the housing area where Joe lived, so I could say goodbye. After talking for a while, Joe held my hand and walked me to the car. I sat in the back seat and looked up at him. Joe bent down and kissed me—my first kiss.

I cried the entire way out of town.

My father shook his head and mumbled, "Oh, the agony of first love."

We had lived in Heilbronn for less than a year. During our stay, I was active in Girl Scouts and had taken the Brownie troop hiking twice. I performed the hula during our dance class recital. I started learning my father's World War II story. Most memorable of all, I had experienced my first kiss—and I thought my world was over as we drove away.

I sat stoically in the back seat of our Volkswagen while my father drove the sixty-two kilometers, or thirty-eight miles, from Heilbronn to Crailsheim over the *autobahn*. As we passed through farmland and small towns, Dad said, "Think of this move as another adventure."

This is not an adventure. It's another place I have to start over again.

TEN

Responsibility

Crailsheim, Germany (1962–1963)

Dad pulled into the parking lot of the temporary officers family quarters on Crailsheim *Kaserne*, the German word for barracks. We stayed there about two weeks until our accommodations readied. Then, we moved into the second floor of a brick apartment building—exactly like every other apartment building in this military housing area—a block away from the manned gate entrance into the work section.

The unit included three bedrooms, one bath, a small kitchen, a dining area, and a living room. A few pieces of furniture—army-is-sue—arrived along with our household supplies, toys, books, and clothing. The rabbit ear antenna presiding on top of a small, black-and-white television procured through the military thrift store needed straightening every time a channel fuzzed out. We also had to rise from our seats and walk across the room to change one of the few stations.

The American Forces Network broadcast system presented news and some movies or American television shows, but, with such poor quality, I preferred listening to Radio Free Europe or my many single or 45 rpm vinyl records on my portable record player. I sang "Take Good Care of My Baby" along with Bobby Vee, "Runaround Sue" with Dion, and "Will You Love Me Tomorrow" with The Shirelles. By the end of my stay in Crailsheim, the song "Go Away Little Girl" by Bobby Vee brought me to tears.

My mother purchased our clothing, food, and household items at the post exchange, the thrift shop, the commissary, or the Class VI store. She only ventured *onto the economy* when my father accompanied her. "Everything we need is right here. Why go elsewhere?" she said.

A chain-link fence separated our housing area from the main post. Although this didn't surprise me, I wondered why we were caged off from the activity there. We had to show our identification when walking through the gate or, if traveling by car, go around to the front entrance to get to the commissary, clubs, and recreation areas. Mike's elementary school was located in the housing area.

All high school students who lived on post, about thirty or forty of us, gathered around 5:00 p.m. every Sunday at the train station or *Bahnhof*. We rode the train to Nürnberg American High School in Fürth, Germany. There we stayed until the following Friday when the buses picked us up after school and dropped us—carrying our laundry—at the train station for our weekly return home. This was, perhaps, the happiest year of my high school life. I felt free—unburdened of my brother, away from parents—yet still in a protected military environment.

Sometimes, a soldier traveled with us on the train as our chaperone, but mostly we stayed together aboard two cars separate from the civilian population. Any misconduct reported to headquarters would get our fathers in trouble.

A regimented and structured dorm life, typical cafeteria-style meals—breakfasts, lunches, and dinners—and a common area separating the girls' and boys' dormitories rendered both security and adventure to my high school life. I learned to share a bath area, to sign in and out whenever I left the building, and to keep my space clean at all times since our hall monitor inspected our rooms daily. Ringing bells indicated times for waking, eating, and studying.

Dormitory Schedule		
Wake Up	6:30 a.m.	0630 hours
Breakfast	7:00 a.m.	0700 hours
School	8:00 a.m.	0800 hours
Sign In	5:00 p.m.	1700 hours
Dinner	6:00 p.m.	1800 hours
Study	7:00 p.m.	1900 hours
(in your room, door open)		
Break (15 minutes)	8:00 p.m.	2000 hours
Study	8:15 p.m.	2015 hours
Lights Out	10:20 p.m.	2220 hours

There were few problems in the dorm, although some students smoked cigarettes while outside. Once, I tried a cigarette on the train and grew terribly ill. When I told my father, he actually turned me over his knee and spanked me! Can you imagine that? Both Mom and Dad smoked. Our house reeked of coffee and smoke. *Do as I say and not as I do.* What kind of parenting was that?

But I never smoked again. As a matter of fact, my stomach still churns every time I smell burning tobacco.

Our sixteenth birthdays signaled the legal age for drinking beer in Germany. However, we, as Americans, could not drink until our twenty-first birthdays. This seemed strange to me. Most of our soldiers were teenagers. They could carry a gun and fight a war but not drink a beer? But since I was not a soldier, I didn't care that much.

Perhaps other students did have beer parties, but I never went to one. Drinking alcohol was commonplace in the military, rarely while on duty. On the other hand, we bought cough medicine—*GI gin*—at the local pharmacy and hid it in our lockers. Sometimes, we took a swig. It packed a buzz. My roommate kept a bottle.

Illegal drugs like marijuana, cocaine, or LSD were not a problem, although an inventive student or two may have created something in chem lab now and then. I walked down the steps from English lit to my social studies class as teachers ran up the steps toward the chemistry lab. The air smelled of rotten eggs. *What is going on?*

The next day, scuttlebutt said someone had cooked up some LSD. Whether that was true or not, I seriously doubted.

School away from home was a lot of fun. I enjoyed my teachers, classmates, and studies, but more than that, I felt free. After classes, my girlfriend and I walked through the back fields to the post exchange or commissary/snack bar. The walk took about thirty minutes there and thirty minutes back, so we didn't stay long, but we felt independent.

I met a senior, Richard Stone, who also lived in Crailsheim. Curly black hair topped his slim body and framed his brown eyes. I didn't care that his lips looked a little strange—he had a cleft palate—and he slurred some of his words. Neither did I care that his father was a master sergeant and mine was an officer.

My parents cared a great deal, and we argued over my dating him.

Rick and I often left the allotted train cars and sat with the locals, so we could be by ourselves without the noise generated by a group of rambunctious teens. We became known as "Stone and Pebble."

During the fifteen-minute break at study time each evening, we met in the combined great area and sat together holding hands. I rested my head on his shoulders. When a girl I'd had a disagreement with ran up to me and started yelling about something I don't recall, I yelled back, but instead of keeping this fight verbal, she hit me.

Rick stood. She backed up. But I began shaking.

I had been fainting since grade school. This dizziness continued through high school, but I had learned to anticipate losing consciousness, and this was one of those times. "Rick," I said, touching his shoulder. "I don't feel well. I need to lie down."

The girl ran off, but Rick got the dorm mother, who escorted me to my room and my bed, where I waited till the shaking stopped.

A few days after this, during my social studies class, I felt the same sensation. I put my head on the half desk in which I sat but still felt as if I would fall onto the floor. Mr. Mueller, our teacher, sent me to the nurse with another student. I rested there without losing consciousness.

Rick appeared. He explained to the nurse about my propensity for falling.

Military doctors continued telling my mother I would outgrow this tendency. I didn't. It wasn't until I turned fifty-five years old that doctors informed me I had multiple sclerosis.

There were many arguments between my parents and me over my dating Richard. We had even discussed the possibility of eloping but could not figure out how to get out of Germany.

In our innocence, neither of us realized the seriousness of our parents' concerns. Dad asked Sergeant and Mrs. Stone to our home to discuss the matter. I was not present during their conversation but was told afterward that Rick and I needed to break up.

"That is not going to happen," I told my parents. "I love him. We're going to get married when we get back to the States." At sixteen, life would be over without him. How could they even think I could go on living if we were separated?

My parents assumed more was going on than really was, so they sent me to the priest on post. His accusations freaked me out. How could the priest think I would do some of the things he talked about?

After my discussion with the cleric, I ran to Rick's home. His parents were out, so we talked in his bedroom and decided he needed to go to college after graduation, and we'd see each other again back in the States. We'd stick together no matter what. Then the song "Go Away Little Girl" by Bobby Vee came on the radio.

Evidently, my parents decided their fears had been unjustified. I was allowed to attend the senior prom that year with Rick. The theme was Harbor Lights. I wore my prettiest knee-length party dress, high heels, and my white faux rabbit fur shawl. My family drove to Nürnberg and stayed at a hotel there, so I could meet Rick and attend the prom at the Officers Club on post. We ate our meal, danced, and then returned to the hotel at curfew—midnight.

Rick's father transferred, and Rick left for the United States and college while I remained in Germany. I listened to my records and sang "The End of the World" along with Skeeter Davis, "Rhythm of the Rain" with The Cascades, and "Blue on Blue" with Bobby Vinton. I stood at our living room window next to the phonograph, singing and crying.

After Rick left, he and I corresponded. He taped a charm to every letter.

"Peggy," my mother said one day while I moped, "where are the letters Rick has been sending to you?"

"In my basket on the shelf in my bedroom."

"Bring them to me."

"No! They are mine."

But as soon as my father returned home, the letters came down from my shelf and were destroyed. I saved the charms and have them today on a bracelet. I've occasionally thought about this high school sweetheart and what happened to him. I like to think he became an important businessman or scholar or politician somewhere. I hope he married, had lots of kids, and lived a happy, fulfilling life.

Many cities in Germany had names I found interesting—like Hamburg in Northern Germany or Frankfurt in Central Germany. And there was also Berlin, then a divided city between West and East but surrounded by East Germany and ruled in the communist way.

All US military centers, including Crailsheim, enacted high-alert protocols when President Kennedy visited Germany in June 1963. We listened to the radio while we ate and heard his speech about how those who loved freedom only needed to visit Berlin to see how a wall was built to separate a nation and keep people in captivity.

"*Ich bin ein Berliner*," the president said, meaning he was a citizen of Berlin. But a resident of Berlin would not have referred to himself as a *Berliner*, the German word for a fried, jam-filled pastry. Some scholars have therefore asserted President Kennedy's famous sentence literally translated into "I am a jelly doughnut."

That summer—and during the school year to come—American students greeted and joked with each other using Kennedy's speech. The instigating student said, "*Ich bin ein Berliner*."

The next replied, "*Ich bin ein Hamburger*."

Another said, "*Ich bin ein Frankfurter*."

Inevitably, someone would say, "*Du bist ein Dummkopf*," meaning, "You are a fool."

I had looked forward to returning to dormitory life at the Nürnberg American High School, but as had happened frequently, Dad transferred. This time, we would move to Bamberg, a city about 164 kilometers, or 102 miles, from Crailsheim. Bamberg, considered a World Heritage Center, was one of the few cities in Germany that had not been bombed extensively or destroyed during World War II.

Moving had become my way of life. At least all my fellow students did the same thing. As my father had once suggested, adapting to new circumstances seemed almost like a new adventure. The adventures I had in Germany have stayed with me as if they happened yesterday.

Military Vacations

Germany (1961–1963)

When military service members volunteer to take the oath and sign their military contract, they agree they will take orders and do what they are told without question while serving their country. They cannot quit or fail to show up for work, nor can they skip the job. Military families understand this concept. However, service members can take vacations called *leaves* for specified periods. During our family's stay in Heilbronn and Crailsheim, Dad requested leave whenever possible and whenever his duties allowed. The military had paid for our family to live in Europe, so we intended to make the most of it.

"Okay, load up," Dad said at the beginning of weekends or three-day holidays, and our family filled our blue 1960 four-door Ford station wagon. Mike and I carried comic books, notebook paper, homework, green plastic toy soldiers, Matchbox cars, and our toothbrushes in backpacks. We also grabbed the Sears Christmas catalog and pillows. Mom neatly folded every item of outerwear— shirts, dresses, and pants—and tucked away socks, underwear, stockings, and swimsuits. She always packed a small cosmetic bag for shampoo, hair spray, lotions, medications, etc. Dad's uniform and suit hung in a long suit bag.

Dad lugged the bags to the car, where Mom arranged them just so, leaving no space unused. We wore our dog tags. Mom carried the family passports, and Dad kept hold of his leave papers. Mom also managed the maps and served as navigator.

We took off for little medieval towns, Renaissance castles, and various cities within Germany—like Stuttgart, Munich, or Heidelberg—or throughout Europe. My parents enjoyed traveling. They wanted Mike and me to explore the world with them, experiencing new cultures—food, festivals, architecture—and histories of foreign lands.

"Where are we going this time?" I asked.

My parents rarely explained their plans. Or, perhaps, I never listened.

It amazed me that we could drive from one country and cross through to another without any problem. I don't remember stopping for customs, but we probably did. We used the unfamiliar money after we exchanged our American cash into the currency of whichever nation we visited. Of course, every country took US dollars.

Mom wanted to see the tulips in Holland. I remember looking out the car window at a very flat, low, green country with nothing in sight but windmills. I had little knowledge of the land of the boy in the story about silver shoes or the writings of Anne Frank or Hans Christian Andersen, so we missed many interesting spots. People wore traditional Dutch clothing and walked to work in their fields wearing wooden shoes. When we entered larger towns, people wore modern clothing.

We visited several villages famous for their flowers and stopped at a hamlet for a cheese festival. Tulip fields in Holland covered acres of land showing row upon row of brightly colored red, yellow, white, orange, purple, and even multicolored varieties. Although we were told tulips have no smell, the air was scented with the floral perfume of lilac and hyacinth.

We didn't stay long in Amsterdam. We got lost driving around the one-way streets over canals. Both the waterways and sidewalks appeared white and empty.

On another trip, we traveled south through Germany and stopped at various medieval towns until we entered Switzerland, where we visited the Rapolds, our friends from Georgia. Nathalie and I took up our friendship from where we left off. She told me that her parents in India sold her when she was little because they could not afford to keep her. While Colonel Rapold had been stationed in India, he bought her and later adopted her.

Shocked at this revelation, I asked how she felt about it.

"Oh," Nathalie said. "I'm happy. I have two families. My new family always treats me like one of their own. They helped my old family. Besides, that was common in India."

My family took our most memorable trip in the summer of 1963. We had entered Italy from Austria and driven awhile toward Rome. Always fascinated with history, geography, and new cultures, I watched out the window and created stories in my head. In some, peasants carried water jars on their heads as early Christians hid from Caesar's wrath. I imagined Roman legions marching these same paths after conquering the Goths. While passing ancient aqueducts, I envisioned enemy tanks rumbling through towns during the two world wars.

Dad turned the car onto a small road in the countryside.

"Al," Mom said for the second time, holding the map on her lap. "This is not the road to Rome."

"All roads lead to Rome," Dad answered.

"No," Mom insisted. "We need to turn around and go to the junction about five klicks back."

"I've been here before," Dad answered quietly.

Turning down a road familiar only to him, Dad became distracted and quiet. He braked, got out of the car, and walked to a small sign on the side of the road.

Ospitale, the sign read.

Sensing a significant story about to unfold, I followed Dad to the edge of a street and down to the railroad tracks a short distance from where Mom and Mike still sat, perplexed, in the car. Dad watched the sky, scanning for something.

"What is it, Daddy?" I felt concerned, for I had never seen my father so melancholy and intent while watching clouds.

Shaking his head, Dad whispered, "I'm looking for aircraft. Guards marched us out here to these tracks for work detail. Occasionally, Allied planes strafed the tracks. We were concerned for our safety, but we were happy whenever we saw our planes. That way, we knew we would eventually win. We would be liberated."

Chills ran up and down my arms despite the summer warmth.

I had known from an early age that my father had been listed as MIA—missing in action—during the war. His parents received a telegram stating that their youngest son was MIA and presumed dead. When Dad returned from the war after being liberated, they had not received any further notice, so when he rang their doorbell the day he came home, my grandmother thought he was a ghost. Two days after his appearance, another telegram arrived, notifying them that he had been a POW—prisoner of war—and was found. In later years, telegrams always upset my grandmother. They returned her to the day the first telegram arrived.

I also knew that Dad's two brothers—and Mom's older brother—had all served and returned without any visible wounds. Like my father, they had not shared or repeated war stories among themselves at home.

Until this visit twenty years later, my dad had not expressed exact details of his capture or treatment to any of us. He had, however, returned to them in his night sweats. Now, my father at last opened up about his experiences.

After a short time passed, without us seeing any aircraft while Dad and I stood alongside the railroad tracks, we walked back to our car and drove past the Ospitale sign. Dad's memories transported him, and us, back to 1944 and the Second World War.

A few minutes later, he parked in front of a large concrete building surrounded by barbed wire.

Dad chuckled and walked around a tiny tree. "Look, Peggy." He pointed to the scrawny, spindly trunk the size of a small birch. "That is the tree I looked at from my window and dreamed of using to escape. I thought it was huge," he mused and then continued more to himself than to me. "I guess it seemed formidable with the barbed wire and machine guns guarding it."

Dozens of local people, young and old, soon surrounded our vehicle. Word that a foreigner had arrived spread through this little town that hadn't changed since the war. A diminutive lady walked up to my father and spoke with him in English. The town's mayor welcomed Dad. We ate a complimentary lunch, and then a delegation escorted Mom and me to the beauty salon, where the same lady who spoke English and happened to be a beautician styled our hair. I felt like I had won on the show *Queen for a Day*.

At Ospitale in Italy

Still showing remnants of swastika markings etched beneath graffiti, the gray, concrete structure that once housed Allied prisoners of war now stood vacant. It had served as the village school before and immediately after World War II. Now, it sat neglected.

Daddy in front of his POW camp, 1963

Walking as if through fog, Dad pointed to the well between two stone walls that separated the building from town. "Here," he said, "we lined up at this well to get our water. If we were lucky, one of the locals tied a loaf of bread to a rope and lowered it into the well. Then we ate the bread with our water."

"Did the guards know?" I asked.

"Probably, but they didn't bother us. When our Red Cross packages came through, we bribed guards with cigarettes or candy bars."

Life in camp must have been horrendous.

The mayor, accompanied by several other men and the beautician, opened the gate to the building and escorted us through the structure. Once inside this school-turned-prison, Dad stopped in front of a closet in the center hallway. Opening the closet door, we found a wooden bench with a hole in its center. This, Dad explained, was *the john*.

"I was small, thin, and a private," Dad remarked while looking into the hole. "It was my job to clean the muck. A guard took me out to the tracks where I dumped it. I didn't think I'd ever get rid of the smell."

My mother, brother, and I followed Dad up steep wooden steps and into a large gray room swept clean and devoid of furniture. Dad stopped, peered at the floor, and said, "This was my spot." Then he grew quiet.

A little later, he added, "The bed bugs were awful. We were always itching, cold, hungry, thirsty, and dirty. They brought in a new man, here." Dad pointed to the floor. "He was wounded. I tried to help. He died."

Dad moved across the room. He stood before the barred window, moving his hands back and forth as if teasing someone. Then he chuckled. "I used to stand here during the day. A young girl who had long pigtails, and her friend, walked by here each morning. I played like I was pulling her braids."

While Dad pantomimed in front of the window, the beautician, who was standing behind, took a shallow breath and placed her hand over her mouth. At that moment, she remembered my dad—she was the friend of the girl he teased. She contacted the girl with the braids, Sylvannia, who happened to live in a nearby town. Our family visited in her home the next day.

Sylvannia was pregnant with her second child when she, her small daughter, my father, my mother, my brother, and I sat around her large dining room table laughing and pantomiming, trying to communicate across time and culture. Sylvannia's husband, a world-famous ski athlete, was away on a skiing trip in the Alps.

Dad explained that a guard named Max agreed to take him to church one Sunday. "When I walked into the church, even the priest seemed shocked. After Mass, another soldier spoke with Max, who then took me to where Sylvannia was standing. She smiled and handed me a box containing cigarettes and bread."

I have sometimes thought about this woman and wondered if I would have been so bold as to help an enemy soldier in time of war.

Our trip to Ospitale twenty years after the war, and the way folks there treated us—their former enemies—helped me develop a profound understanding that people everywhere, regardless of their political ideology or living circumstance, care for each other and come together to help one another in dire circumstances. I learned to try not to stereotype people or judge them by race, culture, or religion. Ospitale taught me that people are basically the same everywhere.

TWELVE

Alert—Possible War

Bamberg, Germany (1963–1964)

When our leave time ended, my family moved from Crailsheim, Germany, to Warner Barracks in the city of Bamberg, where quarters awaited us on the third floor of an apartment building similar to the one we vacated in Crailsheim.

The furniture and household items we had collected arrived a few weeks after we did—minus a television since it had been returned to the rental service before we left. We had a phonograph console and radio. I listened to *The Lone Ranger*, *Bonanza*, and reruns of older shows like those starring Jack Benny and Abbott and Costello as well as various mystery and science fiction clips—whatever was broadcast by American Forces Network.

My family listened to Radio Free Europe when we traveled by car, which we tried to do whenever we could. Often, we heard static. We'd shake our heads and say, "Oh, there go the commies again. They cannot stand free news."

But I wondered what was wrong with our music.

My parents had rented a piano, so when we weren't away exploring, I could practice at home. They hired a German gentleman as my teacher; he played at the Officers Club. Instead of training me with the hated metronome, he wrote the chords of the songs he played at the O Club onto music sheets for me. I found his method easier to learn, and I enjoyed playing "When Irish Eyes Are Smiling," "Over the Rainbow," "Moon River," and "Someday My Prince Will Come."

Our apartment in Bamberg stood catty-corner to the teen club where my friends and I attended activities held on Friday and Saturday evenings. Curfew for military dependents was 9:00 p.m. during the week and 11:00 p.m. on weekends. I never learned what would have happened had I stayed out later. My parents gave me a personal curfew of 10:00 p.m. on Saturday. Neither brat nor soldier walked around the housing area after curfew, and girls rarely walked alone.

Often, the club sponsored chaperoned bus trips to skating rinks, German-American teen gatherings, or the bowling alley. Otherwise, after-school life was limited and monitored. Teen parties, if not scheduled at the club, usually took place in homes where parents assumed responsibility. Movies cost twenty-five cents for children and teens, but the theater shut down at eleven o'clock. Even the Officers Club closed early.

One Saturday evening at the teen club, I watched a group of teenage boys play the time-honored, always available games of table shuffleboard and foosball. The guys whooped and hollered while they played surrounded by giggling girls.

I, one of those giggly girls, centered my attention on a tall fellow sporting a GI crew cut and brown, sparkling eyes. He wore a brown-gray checkered sweater pulled over a tan shirt. He seemed like a nice kid. I remained in the group watching the boys play foosball and rooted for him with each contest. I waited until the last round, and as our group dispersed, I approached him.

"I have to be in the house by ten tonight," I said. "Would you walk me home?"

He looked down at me with those smiling eyes and said, "Curfew's not until eleven."

"I know, but my father says I have to be home by ten. It's dark outside."

"Sure," he said. "My name is Terry."

He walked me home, and we became friends.

Terry was a sophomore and I a junior, but this made no difference. We enjoyed meeting at the teen club, talking, laughing, walking hand in hand with a group of friends, and picnicking on the fields behind the baseball stands. With my last name Greene and his Fields, our friends dubbed us "The Green Fields." Other than sponsored teen events, church activities, and daytime talks at the snack bar on post, we knew of only one appropriate place for a date: the movie theater. But Terry and I had a problem. Dad decided I needed a chaperone—my brother.

"A chaperone?" I screamed. "I don't need a chaperone. I'm sixteen years old."

"Peggy," my mother said. "It gets dark out there, and you never know what may happen."

"I lived in the dorm at school last year. All I had to do was sign out. I didn't need a chaperone then. What do you think will happen? I won't be alone. I'm on a date." My voice rose higher with each statement.

"That's enough," Dad said. "Your brother will be going with you when you are out after dark." My father's tone meant I listened, but I suspected the true reason I had to take Mike was to give my mother a needed break.

Walking with my date to the movie seemed humiliating with a third-grade kid hanging around, especially when we entered the theater, bought him a drink and popcorn, and handed him a quarter to sit up front so we could sit in the back. Then, the little twerp sat down right beside us!

I soon learned how to avoid my chaperone. If I managed to slip away from the house before nightfall for activities at the teen club, I could return after dark as long as I made it back inside the house by ten. This ploy worked on most Friday and Saturday evenings. Once, however, my date and I stayed a little too long talking under the apartment door light downstairs.

Stuff started falling from the sky—*plop*.

A few seconds later—*thump*.

"Ow," Terry said, holding his shoulder. We glanced onto the

ground and found three stones of graduating sizes from pebble to rock. We looked up.

A shadow darted away from the open window directly overhead on the third floor.

"It's my brother," I said. "We'd better go in."

After Terry kissed me at the door to say good night, he hopped down the steps and out into the dark.

I stormed into our apartment ready to confront Mike. The shouting escalated until our father stepped in. My brother had hidden a rock collection under his mattress. He'd waited until I showed up in the parking lot. Then, he'd removed the rocks, aimed, and hit my date. Dad spoke with Mike and confiscated the rocks while I fumed in my room.

"Peggy," Dad said when they emerged, "Mike has something to say to you."

Instead of offering the expected apology, my shamefaced, eight-and-a-half-year-old brother said, "You can't go out with him. You need to marry me."

A bit abashed and stifling laughter, I said, "I'm not going to marry anyone right now. If we could, I'd marry you anytime."

On the evening of November 22, 1963, Mom, Mike, and I walked together up the hill from our apartment to an auditorium just off post but still in the housing area. Mike wore his blue Cub Scout uniform. Mom and I wore dresses. My little brother was due to receive an award onstage that evening, so he joined the other boys behind the curtain. Dad, we knew, would join us after work.

Promptly at 6:00 p.m., 1800 hours in military time, the ceremony began with the placing of the colors, the Pledge of Allegiance, an invocation, and someone explaining why we'd all assembled. Dad entered and sat beside us. Meanwhile, we waited, anticipating the boys coming onstage to receive their awards. Within half an hour after the assembly began and before presentations, a uniformed soldier entered, strode to where we sat, and whispered in my father's ear.

Dad became rigid, took a breath, leaned across toward my mother, and said, "Take the kids home, lock the door, and wait. I have to go."

He left.

A few minutes later, the ceremony ended—prematurely—and another soldier walked onto the stage. "The president has been shot," he announced. "All military personnel, report immediately to your unit. Dependents, return to your quarters and await instruction."

A huge intake of air sounded as people responded to this announcement. Soldiers in and out of uniform stood and quietly left. Women and children looked around, amazed and stunned. Scouts and other participants joined the audience in an orderly, hushed hurry out into the night and toward their homes. No one spoke.

When we entered our apartment, Mom locked the door, turned on the radio, and set about gathering our emergency supplies and our evacuation map. It outlined a route—through France and then over to England—for use if dependent families were ordered to leave the country. I knew that in the trunk of our car we already carried a case of food in the form of K-rations, water, and an emergency kit containing a flashlight, batteries, first aid items, a blanket, and a basic tent called a shelter half.

Mike and I sat on the sofa in the living room, waiting and listening, but my thoughts raced. *How could anyone shoot President Kennedy? What happens now? Who did this?*

The voice on the radio confirmed the unthinkable news. "President Kennedy died at 1:00 p.m. Central Standard Time..."

Immediately after the assassination, everything on post mobilized.

Given the order at the same time, all forms of transportation— tanks, jeeps, and troop trucks—rumbled at once. The sound bellowed like the simultaneous roar of every lion in Africa. Then, they were gone.

Who shot the president? Was it the communists? What shall we do? Are our families safe in Germany, or will we have to leave via the evacuation route?

Few people left their homes. We stayed in our quarters listening to the radio.

Mom received phone calls but told us nothing.

The church filled—even with few men present.

Will we have school on Monday?

After Mass, which was in Latin, the priest promised us the men would return soon. He assured us that no immediate evacuation was scheduled, but he also informed us that all children should stay home from school until further notice.

For three more days, we went about our business as normal— almost. Elementary kids played ball in the park across the street. Teens hung out in parking lots or on the corners. But we all stayed close to home. Everyone, including the German population, seemed in shock and saddened.

In the middle of the night, less than a week after they mobilized, Dad and the soldiers returned. They had been on standby close to the Czech border in case of war.

President Kennedy's death was an important and traumatic event for all of us. It marked the beginning of a long line of tragedies for our government. Lyndon Johnson became our commander in chief, and another conflict, of which we were then unaware, began brewing on the continent of Asia.

We watched President Kennedy's funeral on the television at the visiting officers quarters with Captain Elliot and his family, who had just transferred to Bamberg. Mrs. Elliot mentioned that her brother numbered among the policemen who accompanied the president's motorcade on the day of the shooting.

Soon after Dad returned, we loaded into the car and drove the evacuation route as a trial run. I sat high in my seat and watched as we drove over small streets winding through villages. I saw only one sign in both English and German displaying the words *Evacuation, Fluchtweg*.

Behind the wheel, Dad gave us instructions along the way. "If an evacuation is ordered, place this sign on the dash. Drive along this route in convoy with other dependents and an escort. Military police will be stationed along the route if you need assistance."

I memorized every word Dad said but worried about how we'd fare in a wartime situation. *Will enemy soldiers shoot at our convoy? Will any of us survive a nuclear explosion?*

We drove as far as the border of France, but we did not enter that country before we turned back.

Every morning before dawn, I joined about forty or so high school students who boarded a train for the ride to Nürnberg American High School. All of us "Bambergers" stayed on two cars on that train. We started the school day in study hall and left our last-period class a few minutes early due to the train schedules. Because of this, few of us played any sports or attended sporting events. We returned home each night for dinner. Our school did have football, basketball, baseball, and track teams, but they were not part of my experience.

Terry gave me a lovely watch on a chain, and I wore it around my neck for that year and the next. He and I sat together with a small group of his friends on our weekday commute. But before the end of that school year, his father transferred.

Families are permanent. Friends are temporary.

After Terry left, I spent much of the time on the train practicing shorthand or sitting alone out in the area between cars, thinking, making up stories, and praying. I feared the world would blow up soon. So, being a devout Catholic, I made a deal with myself and God: I would say the Rosary every day and attend Friday Stations of the Cross for six months, and the world would be safe.

I broke the deal, and the world continued much the same.

As a teenager living overseas on guarded military posts without access to television or news reports, I remained unaware of the extent of racial injustice in the United States, the civil rights movement, the Cuban Missile Crisis, or the hostilities in Vietnam. Of course, my father kept informed, and some news traveled by word of mouth, but as a sixteen-year-old—more interested in good grades and boys—I didn't really care about politics and news. I worried only that nuclear war could occur at any time.

In my junior year, I gained more than an academic understanding of my classwork in subjects such as German III, chemistry, home economics, physical education, and shorthand. I developed and added to the fond memories of the teachers who would most influence my teaching—like Mr. Boyd from Heilbronn and now Mr. Mueller from Nürnberg.

Mr. Mueller, my teacher in American history, psychology, and—during my senior year—international relations, sat on his desk while teaching. He taught us how to create an outline, and he joked with us, all the while maintaining our respect.

During the Cold War, Nazi hunters looked for and often found wanted Nazis hiding in plain sight. A rumor started that Mr. Mueller was one of those criminals. Although this was untrue, we had many days of fun at his expense. He played along with us, but he explained that finding those murderers was no joke.

When he decided to marry his kindergarten teacher friend, we held a funeral in his honor, especially after discovering they had spent their honeymoon on separate trips. He laughed along with us. "After all," he said, "she wanted to go to Spain, and I have not seen Russia. Besides, that will give us a lot to talk about." The boys snickered. *Sure, talk about.*

My creative writing and English literature teachers arranged a four-day trip to London for a select group of junior-level students—including me. Approximately sixty of us, excited to be off on our own, boarded a flight from Germany to London with our teacher chaperones. Each student, already assigned a roommate, received the same instructions to always stay with a group. Before the trip, my parents arranged for me and my roommate, Gail, to meet with my cousin's aunt Emily, who lived close to London.

The second night in England, Aunt Emily, wearing her fur coat, met my roommate and me in the lobby of the hotel. She took us for a proper British supper, or *tea*, where we talked about family, interesting things to see, and places to go while visiting. "We have a wonderful array of hearty foods here on the isle," she said and then ordered roast beef with carrots and potatoes. But that was not all. We ate Yorkshire pudding for dessert and chose scones for our next-day treat. Then, Aunt Emily told us to try the fish and chips, trifles, and shepherd's pie while we were there.

"And remember," Aunt Emily said, "if you get lost or need help, always look for a bobby."

Gail and I walked around London in the mist and fog with no particular goal in mind. We rarely bumped into our teacher chaperones, but we always stayed with other students and met up at scheduled times in appointed places. One night we attended the play *My Fair Lady*. Another evening, we met at a movie theater for a Richard Burton film, and the last night, we attended the play *The Sound of Music*.

Each day brought us a new adventure. Watching the Changing of the Guard ceremony at Buckingham Palace, seeing the Crown Jewels in the Tower of London, listening to Big Ben, and riding double-decker buses didn't compare to the time my girlfriend and I chose to ride the London Underground in search of Madame Tussaud's famous wax museum.

"Is this where we get off?" Gail asked.

"I'm not sure, but let's do it anyway," I said.

Wringing our hands because we didn't know where we were or how to get to wherever it was we wanted to go, Gail and I exited the train. We climbed the stairs and emerged into the chilling fog. We looked around at the tall buildings.

Now what?

I remembered Aunt Emily's advice. "Maybe we'd better find a bobby."

"Good day," said a man in a long trench coat. He carried an umbrella and tipped his hat. "May I be of service?"

Giggling, we explained we were lost and needed to find the wax museum.

"Just turn there at the corner. Remember, we drive on the other side of the road, so look to your left and then right. By the by, you might see Sherlock Holmes. He lives over there on Baker Street." The man winked and tapped his umbrella on the concrete.

Gail and I looked at each other with eyes wide. "Really? Sherlock Holmes."

The man chuckled. "How are things in the Colonies?"

Gail and I burst out first in giggles, then with laughter. We, however, watched carefully—just in case Sherlock Holmes should appear.

Once at the wax museum, we met up with several guys from our group. We walked together to our appointed meeting spot, where we attended one of the plays before retiring to our separate hotel rooms.

Although drinking was a familiar pastime for soldiers and their wives in the military, we teenage dependents did not openly imbibe. However, the stewardess on our return trip from Heathrow to Germany presented each of us with a short glass of champagne.

In midflight, our teachers rose and motioned for silence. "In thanks for this wonderful excursion, we tip our glasses to you. No one got lost, in trouble, or had any problems. Congratulations!"

When I returned home, my mother asked how the trip went.

The first thing I blurted out was "I had a glass of champagne!"

I had no intention of driving in Germany. Each time I rode as a passenger, it felt like I was flying close to the ground. Swerving around chickens and livestock, I held onto my beating heart so it wouldn't pound out of my chest. Roads had no speed limits, and the few existing signs were of the international variety. At dangerous curves where buildings obstructed views, mirrors alerted drivers on one side of the road whether any obstructions—like tanks—loomed in the opposite direction. Few teenagers drove off the post.

On military grounds, the speed limit never exceeded 35 mph, or 55 kph. Most teenage dependents did not drive or carry US driver's licenses, which were accepted along with military identification. We had no driver's education in school, so after Dad drove our family on the evacuation route tour, he arranged for a sergeant in his outfit to take me out to the ammo dump and teach me to drive. According to my parents, I would use this skill only in an emergency or while on post for errands to the commissary, post exchange, or clinic.

I didn't object. I wanted to drive whenever I could—until I had an accident.

In reality, I had two. The first happened with the sergeant while I practiced in the ammo dump, a hazardous place, I thought, especially since it was off limits. I missed a curve and slammed into a white fence behind which stood a wire barrier with a warning sign: *Verboten, Live*

Munition. Automobiles of the day lacked seat belts, so hitting the fence jolted us toward the dash when I slammed on the brakes.

The sergeant turned the ignition key off, took a deep breath, put his hand on my shoulder, and said, "I'll drive you home."

I wanted to cry. Instead, I slid over into the passenger seat as he exited the car, inspected the fence, and then got into the driver's side "Don't worry. We'll get that fixed. There's no problem with the car."

My driving career is over. What would have happened if I'd hit a bomb or something?

That night, I told my Dad.

He said, "Get back up on the horse."

Once my training ended—after I studied the driver's manual, passed the written test and took the driver's test with the sergeant, and was given a certificate—Mom allowed me to drive on post for groceries. Without her present, passengers were forbidden.

During the summer of 1964, I aimed the car into a parking space in the lot by the post exchange.

SCR—R—APE.

I stomped the brake, pulled the automatic shift lever stick into park, laid my head on the steering wheel, and sighed. *Oh geez. What do I do now?*

My hands shook as I opened the driver's door, stepped onto the asphalt, and shut the door. I walked around to the side where I hit the parked car to look for damage. Sure enough. A long scrape marred the other car's door. I don't recall what kind of damage—if any—appeared on my car, but I worried over the evidence of my error. *Don't move the car. That would be leaving the scene of an accident. I'll have to wait for a while. Maybe the driver will come out and tell me everything is fine. No, no he won't. Maybe I could leave a note. Yes, a note.*

> I'm sorry I hit your car. Please call my
> father, Captain Greene, at 555-0100.
> Peggy Greene

I tucked my note of confession under the car's windshield wiper and walked toward Dad's office. I started out with swift steps, but my feet slowed as my mind imagined distressing scenes. *How can I pay for the damage? Will my father be demoted? Will I go to jail?*

By the time I neared Dad's workplace, I changed direction. I turned toward the chapel and walked into the church. One of the pastors must have seen the tears about to slip from the corners of my eyes behind my glasses. He approached and spoke to me.

"Are you all right?" He led me to a pew.

"I don't think so," I stammered. "I just had an accident in the car, and I'm afraid to tell my father."

I do not remember how he responded, but I do remember crying. When I looked up, I saw my dad standing erect in his uniform at the door of the chapel listening to this pastor's words. My father shook his head and walked slowly toward me.

"Oh, Daddy. I'm so sorry," I cried.

He took me into his arms.

Nothing more was said, and my driving experiences in Germany ended.

This dandelion had been grounded.

THIRTEEN

Cuisine, Customs, and Castles

France (1964)

Dad received another mysterious visit from the past similar to the one in Heilbronn. This time, the connection rang via the telephone. He didn't explain anything to my brother and me at first, but our parents soon spoke excitedly about traveling to France to visit Dad's old war buddy, Jean Bergis de Courgevaux.

"We're going to Fra-ance. We're going to Fra-ance," Mike chanted.

The little kid doesn't even know what that is. I stacked my pillow behind me and settled into my space by the window. *Ooh. Paris.* I nearly swooned.

Dad had requested and received a twenty-one-day leave as well as his normal two-day weekend, so we had almost a month of travel ahead. He drove us through the *Kaserne* gate, down the road through Bamberg, and onto the two-lane highway toward Aschaffenburg. We then passed Frankfurt and saw a place called Worms. *Really?*

Fatigue set in after three hours in the car with Mike hopping from one side to the other across the back seat. Fortunately, Dad liked to stop along the way at what Germans called a *Gasthaus*, a place along the road or in a town where travelers could rent a room or rest with access to drink and food. Waitresses wearing traditional attire served beer, bratwurst, schnitzel, sodas, sauerbraten, stroganoff, roulade, spätzle, and homemade *Kartoffelsuppe*, or potato soup.

I liked spätzle, a type of noodles that looked like curled shells. When spätzle touched my tongue, the taste—not crunchy, sweet, sour, or spicy, just a bit buttery and smooth—along with the delicious, lightly sautéed or fried veal cutlets called schnitzel, sent my mind into another world.

Gasthaus bratwurst, on the other hand, gave me a burst of energy. Just greasy enough with its bun filled with sauerkraut, this dish was one of my favorites in Germany. It would have been wonderful if I had been allowed to drink beer with it. People of all ages in Germany drank beer—but Dad wouldn't let me, so even though I wanted it, I had to settle for Coke.

I learned a different custom when at gasthauses with my family. The waitress left a white receipt on the table, so I picked it up. I wanted to see how much our food cost.

Dad smiled, winked, and said, "Thank you. Are you paying the bill?"

Stupefied, I put the receipt down.

My father chuckled. "Whenever you pick up the bill, that indicates you will pay."

Dad and I always tried to use our limited German. He'd raise his hand, finger in the air, summoning the waitress for our bill. He'd say, "*Bezahlen bitte*. You please pay." The correct way of asking for the bill was "*Ich möchte bitte zahlen*. I would like to pay, please" or "*Können Sie mir bitte die Rechnung bringen?* Could you please bring me the bill?" But "*Bezahlen bitte*" always worked.

Germany, the first foreign country in which I lived, became a special place for me. I had ancestors who settled in America from Germany as well as a need to study another language in high school. At that time, I thought everyone should learn the language of the country in which they lived. However, once we entered France, I realized there were different languages in countries throughout Europe, but everyone seemed to understand English.

Dad often said, "If they want my money, they'll speak my language."

Not sure I agree.

Back in the car, borders between Western European countries appeared open like those between states in the United States.

Sometimes, along the road, there would be a small house with a policeman or two checking passports, but that was rare. If we had flown or trained or entered by sea, we would have cleared customs.

I asked my father if we could continue on to Spain. He told me he could not.

"Could we go to Portugal?"

"Yes, but not through Spain." Apparently, the military and the American soldiers were not allowed to enter Spain at the time.

We were driving somewhere in France between the border and Paris when something clunked, then dragged, and clunked again. Black smoke appeared through our back window. Dad pulled over. We all exited the car. Without saying anything, Dad inspected our automobile and then walked back down the road from which we had come.

"What's going on?"

"I don't know, Peggy. Hush," Mom said.

Mike ran behind Dad. The car seemed fine, so Mom and I rolled the windows down, left the doors open, and waited inside.

A while later, Mike and Dad walked up behind us carrying pieces of the muffler.

Using wire stowed in the back, Dad attempted to hook the muffler under the car again, but within a short time, it fell off onto the road. We needed to find a gas station or Ford dealership somewhere.

There were no dealerships.

Driving slowly, we stopped at a small shop with a gas pump out front. Mike jumped out with Dad. Mom and I sat quietly in the car. I continued reading my book.

Dad spoke and pantomimed with two gentlemen wearing dirty dungarees who often wiped their faces with oily rags. After much discussion back and forth getting louder and louder, the workmen shook Dad's hand, pointed him toward a nearby building, took the car keys, and walked into their office.

"They'll find the parts and put it back together by tomorrow morning," Dad told us.

Although the drive from Bamberg to Paris should have taken just eight hours, with our stops—and now this muffler problem—we chose to spend the night in a youth hostel where military personnel could find beds, a restroom, and something to eat cheaply.

We walked, carrying our suitcases and backpacks from the gas station into an old four-story building. We entered an outside elevator made like a steel cage that clacked its way up the flights and deposited us on a landing. There we opened a wooden door and stepped inside a long, dingy hall. Dad signed us in at a table, someone pointed to another door, and we found a long, open room with cots and curtain dividers between spaces. We took a space on the left, close to the common restroom.

Baffled as to why my mother would allow us to stay in such a poor place, but realizing we probably had no choice, I said nothing. Mike ran around checking everything out.

"Hey, Peggy," he yelled. "What's this?"

Mike had wandered into the restroom area. I followed. A white, porcelain, circular contraption slightly shorter than the toilet, with a faucet sticking up from a hole in the center, sat next to the commode. Mike flicked the switch, and water squirted up.

"Gee, I don't know. Let's ask Mom."

She told us it was a place for men to pee. At the same time, she admonished Mike by saying "And you cannot use it."

The next day, before we drove on to Paris, the Frenchmen congratulated each other over their hard, overnight work creating a homemade muffler and installing it on the big American automobile. A man who spoke English stood with the French mechanic. He told my father they were happy to show the American that only the French could create such a fine muffler, and because Americans had done so much for the French winning World War II, they would not charge much. And they didn't.

There it goes again—World War II. Didn't that happen twenty years ago?

In Germany, it had seemed remembrances of this war appeared everywhere. Some buildings and entire sections of cities still contained rubble. Going to school in Nürnberg and passing the stone building where the trials of Nazi criminals, who happened to be soldiers just like my father—well, maybe not just like him—occurred, brought attention to this conflict, especially since Nazi hunter Simon Wiesenthal continued searching for Holocaust guards.

We had visited Dachau and learned about the atrocities committed against the Jewish people. When we lived in Heilbronn, we toured mines where stolen art had been discovered after the war. I now knew some of Dad's POW story from the trip we took to Italy the year before, but I didn't understand its significance and how it would affect our family in the years to come.

I hadn't even been a glint in my father's eye back then. Although World War II had ended, the Cold War had begun with nuclear annihilation possible. *Will this world ever understand? Will I?*

Almost seventeen at the time, of course, I just wanted to get to Paris. Which we did.

Cars streamed down the Champs-Élysées, around the Arc de Triomphe. It seemed everyone in the entire world wanted to operate a car and squeeze into someone else's territory. Even with this congestion, we saw no accidents and heard few sirens. The map lay on my mother's lap as she spotted street signs and directed Dad's driving. I watched out the side window and marveled at the number of people strolling down the street proliferated with outdoor cafés.

"Let's go to the Louvre," I suggested. "I want to see the *Mona Lisa*."

Everyone in the car felt exhausted, but we drove toward the Louvre. The building, in 1964, looked like a fortress. It was brown with heavy soot, and it was closed. I sat back, disappointed. *I'll never see the* Mona Lisa.

Meanwhile, Mom and Dad held a quiet conversation about finding a hotel, eating dinner, and going out that evening. I listened intently.

"Let's stop at the USO, get something to eat, and find a place to stay for the night," Mom said.

"Then we can go out." Dad smiled.

"I'd like to see the cancan," Mom said.

"Mike can stay by himself. Peggy's old enough."

Yes, yes. The cancan. Please. I didn't get to see the Mona Lisa.

"No," Mom said.

I crossed my fingers. *Maybe Mom will change her mind.*

We had something to eat and then lodged at a suggested hotel much better than the hostel in which we stayed the night before. Mom did not change her mind. Perhaps to pacify me, they bought me a souvenir doll of my choice.

Then, Mom and Dad went out.

I'll never see the Mona Lisa *or the cancan.*

The next day, we walked by the Seine River. We marveled at the Eiffel Tower and Notre Dame Cathedral. Mike and Dad loved the gargoyles; Mom and I enjoyed seeing the stained glass rose window. We purchased souvenirs and then drove to the Palace of Versailles for a tour. *Amazing.*

With much more to see, our rendezvous with Dad's buddy somewhere in Southern France fast approached. Disappointed once again, I pouted in the back seat while we drove through the French countryside, ignoring all the wonderful sights we passed.

We traveled what seemed like a long time between stops. My brother whined for the umpteenth time. "Are we there yet?"

The Greene Family in Paris—Daddy, Michael, Mommy, and Peggy

"Almost." Mom draped her map over the back seat. "We have one more inch to go."

That *inch* took forever. The winding, two-lane roads of France, although quite clean, seemed to stretch on and on through medieval towns, places still wrecked. Some spots only contained stone chimneys where houses once stood. Sheep, a few cows, and a horse or two munched grass in pastures. We passed plains of scrub brush and a few trees, with small, distant farm buildings and silos along the way. Finally, Dad drove into a little town, parked along the square, and announced, "We're here."

Where we were, I could not tell. One town looked the same as another.

Mr. Jean Bergis de Courgevaux held Dad in a bear hug. Mr. Bergis was a large man in that he was bigger than Dad's five feet nine inches and much wider—but built like an ox. He and Dad had shared some harrowing experiences and obviously wanted to hunch together for remembering. So, Mrs. Bergis and Mom spent their time sitting on the second-floor balcony of our ancient yet clean hotel while the men shared beer and cheese downstairs.

Naturally, I had to take the three little kids outside—my brother, the Bergis boy about the same age as Mike, and the Bergis girl, a little older. They ran everywhere—right in the middle of the nearly empty streets, around fountains, behind buildings. The only words I remembered from my French class back in junior high were *non* and *serviette*. However, saying "no napkin" didn't help. The boy took to calling me "*Non*" whenever he wanted to show me something.

After a day or two in this town, we hopped into our cars and drove out to the country again. When we stopped in a small town, Dad rushed into a restaurant, looked at the menu, and then took us inside. Mr. Bergis arrived, looked at the listed options, and said something in French. The waiter brought a different menu.

"You need to be careful," Mr. Bergis told my father. "The French are crafty. There are two menus. One for Americans and one for the rest of us."

Lunch—actually, every meal for the French—was a three-hour affair. *It's a wonder they get anything done,* I thought.

First, the waiter brought little bowls of water with parsley for washing our fingers. Then, the first course came like an appetizer they called *hors d'oeuvres*—tiny bits of strange-sounding foods like *bruschetta duet* or crab-and-avocado toasts. Before or with the hors d'oeuvres, the waiter may have served an *aperitif*, a small or not-so-small glass of liquor like Lillet with a twist of orange or sweet vermouth. The second or third course, depending upon how much we wanted, was usually some type of seafood like shrimp or crab cakes. Then, we ate a small dish of lemon or lime sorbet to clean the palate. After this delicious, fruity ice, the main dish of meat or poultry was served with vegetables but no starches. Next, upside down from our point of view, came the salad, which usually had a vinaigrette dressing. Finally, the waiter brought to the table a cheese-and-fruit plate on a wooden board followed by a dessert and a demitasse café — very strong coffee.

Wow. No wonder the French eat for such a long time before their afternoon nap. I wonder how long it takes to cook such a meal.

I tried several new foods like avocado, artichoke, and eggplant. But Dad's leave time didn't allow for lingering over every meal.

We stayed in that town several nights before we loaded up to follow Mr. Bergis and do some castle shopping.

That's right. Mr. Bergis wanted to buy a castle. It seemed he had become quite political after the war and partnered with Charles de Gaulle, the famous hero of the French Underground during World War II and later the undisputed leader of France until 1969. Aside from inheriting money, Mr. Bergis had built a multibillion-dollar company, so he wanted to add to his real estate.

Mrs. Bergis explained, "Castles are difficult to maintain and expensive to renovate, so we only tour those on sale from personal owners who have already renovated them for family use — with modern plumbing, heat, and light — but have also maintained a part of each structure in its original form, so it could be used in the tourist industry."

We rose in the morning, ate cheese and fruit around a table, and loaded ourselves into the two cars. Sometimes, Mike rode with the Bergis family, and Mrs. Bergis rode with us. She gave Dad instructions. Tall and slim with brown hair, she smiled often. But when we came to one town, she grew very sad and quiet. Her eyes clouded. "I was a young woman during the war," she said. "I took a train out to this country area one afternoon and watched the Nazis herd all the Jews from this town into a church in the center of town. Then, they burned the church down. The train passed by quickly, but I'll never forget watching that smoke and hearing the screams."

My imagination immediately took hold of her sorrow. I listened to cries and screams, saw the flames, and smelled the smoke. I mourned with her and wondered how people could do those things to other people. We rode quietly for a while.

It seemed to me that castles, or parts of castles, cropped up everywhere. The only one I remember well stood on top of a little hill surrounded by a small hamlet that, in turn, was surrounded by a stone wall and a moat. We turned from the highway onto a one-lane gravel road and drove toward that wall. The empty moat—lined with well-clipped green grass—served as the first defense when various feudal lords fought with each other more than five centuries ago. Two stone towers stood beside this road and behind the moat where there once had been a drawbridge. Locals must have kept this place up out of pride because it had no graffiti and only a few missing bricks, although many areas had been cemented. People obviously lived in the quaint village houses, but I saw none. *They must be tending the manor*, I thought. *Where are the cars?*

We left our automobiles at the bottom of the hill and walked up stone steps to a gravel courtyard. Evidently, the owners knew we were coming because they met us in there and shook hands with Mr. Bergis. Our tour began while they spoke in French. Occasionally, the woman took my mother and me aside and spoke in English.

The first floor was on concrete. There was no dungeon. The tour showed a typical family home—a kitchen with a stove and an oven, a refrigerator, a sink with faucets, and a wooden table surrounded by four chairs. Further inside, we saw two bedrooms with contemporary furniture, an up-to-date bathroom, and a great room that served as a study, living area, and playroom. Although the walls were obviously solid rock, windows appeared modern on that first floor.

"Would you like to see the *real* castle?" the lady asked. "We restored it to the specifications we found on old manuscripts. But the furniture was gone and the upholstery rotted, so we purchased similar items of the same period. We prefer not to replicate with designed goods."

People back during the days of knighthood must have had very long reaches because the stone stairs were difficult to climb, steep and high. The staircase inside the walls was not stable, so we used the stone steps outside and entered the large bedroom hall directly from those steps.

Window casings were quite large and high—almost to the ceiling. Each pane appeared cloudy. Perhaps no one had washed them lately. The sun barely shone in. Torches hung on the walls. The electricity had not been established as yet. There was no heat or air conditioning.

One high bed piled with quilts and pillows sat in the center of this gigantic room. Beside the bed, there was a wooden stool from which people could climb onto it. The mattress sat on ropes tied together. *Certainly, the princess would not be able to feel a pea.* A small wooden table on the side of the room held a round, porcelain bowl and a white pitcher for water. A pot sat beside the bed, showing that the lord of the manor could use the pot and servants would empty it in the morning.

That was the entirety of this castle's furnishings. Other rooms, swept clean, waited for renovation.

We toured several other castles. I had postcards, but they have all disappeared over the years. Today, while searching "castles in France" on the internet, I discovered people are still buying and selling French castles. I would not want to live in one, for sure. They are old, cold, and barren.

As our time ran out and Dad had to plan on leaving, the Bergis family took us to a midsize town for the night. We could not find suitable housing, so Mr. Bergis drove to a convent. After he spoke with the person in charge, Mother Superior, it was decided that the family could stay at the convent in exchange for a ride to the train station several miles away for this nun and a companion.

Oh, great. I don't see the Mona Lisa. *I can't see a cancan. I traipse around looking at ugly, cold castles for sale, and now I have to sleep in a cell with a bunch of old ladies. Cool.*

It *was* cool.

One of the younger nuns, dressed in a black habit secured by a black waist rope where her rosary hung, escorted Mom and me to Mother Superior's room. This young nun wore a black veil with a white coif around her face and a white collar where her cross necklace hung. She wore comfortable black shoes and a smile. She clicked the electric lights on as she entered the room and walked toward the room on the left.

"Welcome. The restroom is here. It is used by all the sisters. When you use it, please flick this switch down and then back up when you are finished," the nun said in English. Then she left.

A cell? Well, the room may have been called a *cell*, but in reality, it was a rather large, sparsely furnished room with gray, concrete-looking walls about one and a half stories high and with small windows above probably meant for ventilation. Electric lights along the wall about six feet up from the floor, a table lamp on a desk, and another on a table beside the bed brought dull illumination into the room. Centered above the oversized bed—with mattress, box spring, and lots of covers and pillows—a crucifix provided the only wall decoration. *Talk about a serene lifestyle.*

Once we clicked the switch in the restroom, bright lights illuminated many sinks, small mirrors, shelves, and several restroom stalls as well as a large communal shower. Everything sparkled.

We heard no noise and slept wonderfully well. The night ended too soon.

In the morning, we packed up and met the men in the parking lot. Mother Superior and another nun holding several packages joined us. Mother Superior spoke English. As we drove them to the town to catch the train, we passed a large fortress-looking monastery on the right.

"During the war," Mother Superior told us, "all the men were rounded up and hung."

"Were they Jewish?" I asked.

"No, dear. They were Catholic students."

Oh, that war! How can people treat other people like that? Why do men have to be so cruel? What secret do Dad and Mr. Bergis share about the war?

Many years later, my father wrote their story.

In 1944, Dad had been transferred from his original POW camp to an Italian town named Mantova where a larger camp existed mostly of British prisoners. Word circulated that the Germans, losing the war, wanted to transport all prisoners to Germany. Naturally, the prisoners didn't want to go, so while in a separate compound awaiting transport, a group organized to attempt an escape. The only Frenchman, Jean Bergis, and the only American, Albert Greene, banded together.

Buses arrived for transport. The escape group moved themselves so they could all board the same bus. The plan was for whoever sat near the driver and the three guards to jump them while another man stopped the bus. They would all take off for the hills in different directions. Jean and my father would stick together.

Eight buses formed the convoy—three in their front and four behind. Each vehicle changed position now and then. Eventually, the buses in their rear passed them up. They were at the end of the column. Jean asked the Englishmen if they were ready, but they said no. It was too risky.

"Jean and I were very angry at the damn Limeys," Dad wrote.

That night, Allied planes strafed the convoy. The buses stopped. Prisoners and guards ran to the side of the road. "We could see the dust kicked up by the .30-caliber bullets. No opportunities for escape presented until daybreak," Dad continued.

The buses stopped in Trento, where the prisoners quartered on the fifth floor of a large building. When nighttime closed in, they were loaded on buses again. Mr. Bergis and my father dropped the Englishmen and joined a group of Frenchmen to aid in their escape.

This time, the prisoners made their way into a particular bus that had its back window already broken. The plan was to wait until that bus was last in the line, jump the guards, take their guns, and run for their lives.

After traveling for a few hours, Dad asked Jean if he was ready. Jean said he was not.

"The guards in the back were asleep, so I took one of their guns and again asked Jean, but he again said no, so I put the gun down," Dad wrote.

When Jean said he was ready, the guard woke up, so they lost the opportunity to escape. The buses pulled up to their final destination after driving through the Alps and into Austria.

I asked my father why they kept saying they were not ready.

"Peggy," Dad said, "there were machine guns on the top of every bus. If we had tried, there would have been a massacre."

I'm glad they didn't try. If they had, both Jean and my father would have joined the 550,000 Frenchmen and 418,500 Americans who died in the war. Neither my brother nor I would have been born; subsequently, none of our children or grandchildren would have lived.

Years later, Dad told my brother that Jean Bergis de Courgevaux had asked our father if he were really mad at him for telling him he was not ready for the escape attempt. Mike reported to me that our father said, "Yeah, I was madder than hell—until I saw the reflection on that cliff we passed of the machine gun nest of krauts on top."

Sadly, before Dad transferred back to the United States from Bamberg the year after our trip, he received another telephone call, this time from Mrs. Bergis. Jean Bergis de Courgevaux had shot himself in the head committing suicide. It seemed his accountant had lost most of Jean's fortune, and he couldn't continue on without it.

As the daughter of a soldier who experienced these unusual adventures during vacations when my father took leave, I became a more sensitive, serious, strong, and sincere student of cultures, history, psychology, and sociology. Like the dandelion, I stood strong among the thorns, remained steadfast, and grew.

FOURTEEN

Senior Year Skirmishes

Bamberg (1964–1965)

*F*inally, I'm a senior—class of '65. College next.
College next?
Where am I going? How will I get there? What will I study?

Nowhere in my thoughts was *How will I pay for it?*

Oh, well. There's lots of time. I have a whole year left in school.

My senior year started the same as the past three. We Bambergers entered a gray military bus every morning before dawn and exited at the *Bahnhof*, the railway station. There, we shivered on or by the tracks in the cold until a whistle blew and a light sped into the station. We lined up properly, one after the other, and climbed aboard the train. We entered two reserved cars, stowed our strapped books or briefcases overhead, and sat

Peggy Greene,
class of 1965, Nürnberg
American High School

with friends. As the train chugged the hour or so toward Nürnberg *Bahnhof*, we watched the sun come up over the quiet German countryside. The air warmed a little by the time we had boarded and then emptied an additional gray bus from the *Bahnhof* to the Nürnberg American High School in Fürth. We arrived wide awake and ready for anything.

First stop for us Bambergers: study hall. But what for? If we hadn't finished our work at home or on the train, our teachers had assigned too much. Naturally, with a bus full of incoming teenagers who had nothing to do—including a handful of robust guys who wanted only to disrupt class—the teachers on study hall duty streamed in and out before the bell rang for the second-period class, which started about fifteen minutes after our arrival.

Just like back in the States, we kids walked the halls to and from class and sat at half desks where we took notes as our teachers lectured about stuff in which we were not particularly interested. Girls wore knee-length skirts with blouses tucked in or dresses with cardigan sweaters flung over our shoulders. Boys, who looked a lot like men, wore dress pants with shirts tucked in—no cowboy boots, belt buckles, or hats allowed in school. Girls' hair hung low with curls or in ponytails or teased into a bouffant style. The guys, of course, sported GI haircuts. Only one fellow was sent to the office—and his father was notified—because he appeared with a Mohawk haircut. The next time I saw him, he was bald.

During the end of the first semester, the girls on our train car debated about our school attire. "What do you think will happen if we wear slacks?"

"How about shorts?"

"Can we get away with it?"

We didn't know, but after much giggling, we decided to try.

On the designated day of the *Great Pants Showdown*, I wore my kelly green slacks and a white blouse. Unfortunately, the test group was smaller than I'd counted on. Only two other girls appeared on the train wearing slacks. We sat nervously through our classes all day.

In my final class period, I breathed a sigh of relief—until a note came to the classroom.

"Miss Greene," my teacher announced, "please go to the office."

Oh, no. It's the pants. I should never have worn pants. I will never in my entire life wear pants again.

I entered the principal's office. A teacher smiled at me as she slid papers into cubbyholes and motioned for me to take the chair beside the principal's closed door.

Whatever the stern, young principal told me has been lost. I only remember that he said nothing about my attire, and he summoned neither of the other girls to his office.

Although relieved by my escape from reprimand, I still wanted to do something more daring than assert my choice of clothing. After all, this was my last year in school.

I tried chewing gum regardless of the rules, but that wasn't much fun while wearing braces. Then, I argued myself into another idea.

I've never skipped class. I could do that.

But I like all my classes. Why would I want to skip one?

Well, I'm not real fond of PE.

So, I deliberately left my gym clothes in the locker. I gripped my notebook and social studies text as if my life depended on them. My feet dragged through the halls until the bell sounded. Class had begun.

Now what?

I rushed into the girls' restroom. When the halls quieted, I walked out and down the steps and wandered around. Not even teachers hung out after the bell sounded.

There's nothing to do. This isn't cool.

I spent the rest of that forty-five minutes huddled in an alcove corner.

So much for skipping class.

The *in-group* consisted of popular girls—bubbly, cheerleader types—surrounded by guys who were great students or handsome or jocks. And then, there were the rest of us. Although I preferred sitting alone on the train, a group of four of us—three boys and me—developed a liking for each other. We hung out together at the teen club and played blackjack, without money, on the train after school. As friends, we never dated, although I had a crush on one of the three. I discovered later that, although he didn't like me in that way, one of the other boys did.

Thus passed the days of my senior year, except for anticipating three significant events to come. The seniors' class trip, the school prom, and our graduation were all scheduled for the last three months of the academic year—April, May, and June. Meanwhile, the guidance counselor spoke with each of the seniors about our plans for the future.

"Margaret," she said, "your SAT scores are good. You are on the honor roll, and your interest shows you want to attend college. Where would you like to go?"

"I don't know of any schools in particular. But my family is from New York, so perhaps I should apply somewhere there."

"Perfect." She handed me papers to complete for New York University and Berkeley in White Plains.

Knowing nothing about either school, I decided I'd go ahead and apply. I wrote my essay, and I had taken the SAT and other tests required, so I waited for news. Dad told me he'd pay for tuition, but I'd have to find scholarships and grants to help out. My thoughts were not on any after-graduation issues—they were still on high school. *There's time*, I decided.

Mr. Mueller, my social studies, psychology, and international studies teacher, organized a once-in-a-lifetime trip to Berlin for us. My classmates acted as excited and raring to go as I felt. I couldn't wait as I heard all the arrangements he'd made.

Berlin! Imagine visiting East Germany!

I ran into the house after returning from school and showed my folks the permission slip. Expecting an immediate reply, I asked, "Please, can I go?"

My parents said nothing.

All weekend, I looked on the table, but the slip lay there still unsigned. Monday morning, the paper disappeared.

"Mom, I need the permission slip for Berlin. Where did it go?"

"Your father has it."

At school, all we talked about was the upcoming trip to Berlin.

At dinner, Dad looked directly into my eyes. "Peggy, you cannot go to Berlin."

"Why?" I shouted. "Everyone else is going. I'll be the only senior not allowed."

"I'm sorry, Peggy. You cannot go."

And that was that.

No one at home said anything about the trip for several days, but I seethed inside. *Even the colonel's son is going. The only reason we're here is because of Berlin. Everyone else can go—but not me. Why not me? What can I do to change their minds?*

Slowly, as Friday approached, the idea for a plot hatched.

Our family went to the Officers Club for dinner on Friday nights. *Dad won't possibly be able to say no with all those people around us.*

We ate an enjoyable meal, and I waited for the beginning of the music and dancing portion of the evening. Then, I pulled out an additional permission slip and laid it on the table.

I smiled at my father. "Daddy, I have another slip you can sign so I can go with my class on the senior trip."

"To Berlin?" He looked at me.

"Yes."

"Peggy..."

"We cannot let you go," Mom interjected.

"Why?"

"It's too dangerous," my mother said. "I had a dream that you were kidnapped and we couldn't find you."

I looked at my father.

He shook his head. "You cannot go."

Furious, I jumped up from my seat, yelling, "I can't go because of a dream? This is not fair." I turned and ran from the room.

My mother's refusal threw yet another stone into the pile I had been building against her over the years.

Many years later, my father informed me he had been in charge of security in the area. His superiors had determined I could neither fly over East Germany nor enter Berlin. If anything happened to me, security could have been compromised.

And so, I sat alone and brooded in various junior classes while the seniors enjoyed their adventures in Berlin.

After their trip, most of the senior girls talked about the upcoming prom. Many had steady boyfriends or dated soldiers. I did not.

I waited for the boy I liked to ask me to the prom. Girls didn't ask for dates. The guys did. On the train one day, that boy whom I liked handed me and everyone else an invitation to his birthday party. *This is it. He'll ask me for sure.*

The evening of his party, I wore my blue flowered shirt-dress that showed my figure, and I teased my hair into a stylish bouffant. I walked with others to his home in Bamberg, where it seemed the whole post was in attendance. I danced and flirted, but he stayed beside a junior high girl the entire time. My hopes were dashed. When curfew struck, he left with the girl, and another friend walked me home.

Time shortened as my concern about getting a date for the prom grew, so I took matters into my own hands.

One day, I happened to be speaking with another senior, a fellow with whom I shared a class. We'd been friends since living in Crailsheim. He confided he had no prom date.

So, I said, "Would you like to go?"

His face lit up.

I had missed out on Berlin, but I had solved the dilemma of having no date for the prom, and I looked forward to going with this good friend. At last, both the prom and my graduation seemed not only possible but close at hand. We needed only to arrange how my date, who still lived in Crailsheim, and I, who lived in Bamberg, would meet to attend the prom at our school in Nürnberg.

And, of course, I needed a dress.

My mother designed and sewed my first long gown from faux silk and chiffon. The sleeveless bodice of white, silky material featured a high neckline. The skirt, with tucks in the waist, flowed naturally with an overcast of green chiffon. My dress, although homemade, looked flattering even before the final stitches were in place.

"Peggy, stand on this stool. I need to finish the hem," Mom said.

I smiled and stood still, anticipating my prom and looking forward to the upcoming graduation ceremony. We'd already planned to follow it with a little dinner in my honor at the Officers Club.

Mike ran through the room, the door opened, and Dad walked in.

"The dress looks nice," he said, but his next words startled me. "Get down off the stool." He removed his hat, pulled out a chair, and sat.

Uh-oh. What happened?

Mom said, "Go hang the dress in the closet. Be careful. There are pins along the hemline." She closed up the black chalk puffer she'd been using, boxed up the extra straight pins, and picked up the stool. I walked into my room and changed.

Dad remained silent at the table until Mike sat on the floor and Mom pulled out a chair. I perched on the side of the sofa. We all waited. I wondered what earthshaking news Dad was going to tell us.

"I've been transferred again," he said.

"We're moving?" Mike shouted.

Mom didn't respond.

"When?" I asked.

"Soon," Dad said. He placed a folder containing his orders on the table and pushed them forward so Mom could see. She didn't pick them up.

"When?" I repeated, already on my feet beside the sofa, breathing deeply, waiting for the rest. "Before graduation?"

"I'm afraid so. You'll have to take your finals early."

Dumbstruck, I repeated, "Finals...early?"

"I'll call the school tomorrow to arrange that."

"But the prom is less than a month away," I whined.

Finally, Mom stepped in. "Can you delay the move until after graduation?"

Dad shook his head. "You know I asked. If you want to stay here alone for a few weeks that would be fine, but I think it's better we all go together. You and I can talk about this later."

Fine. Dandy. My teenage mind could take no more. "I won't go. I have a date for the prom. Mom made my dress. I couldn't go to

Berlin, and now I can't go to my prom?" I stomped out of the room, slammed my bedroom door, grabbed the koala bear from my bed, and threw it across the room.

How dare he do this to me. Nothing ever goes right. We're always moving when something important happens.

Reason found no room in my seventeen-year-old, short-circuited brain. I stayed curled up with Koala and Raggedy Ann. I pounded my pillow now and then. I didn't cry. I knew I had no choice. My life had no choice.

At dinner, Dad explained further. "We'll be leaving together. We have three weeks to prepare. I'll talk with the principals tomorrow and arrange your transfers."

"Where are we going?" I asked.

"Louisiana. A place called Fort Polk."

Again…we're moving…again.

When I saw my prom date in class, he smiled, but then I told him the bad news. He looked at the floor, quiet for a second, and then shook his head. Being a military dependent himself, he understood about sudden changes.

After all Dad's transfers, Mom had become a great organizer and packer. She set about the task of arranging the house. She sorted through furnishings, clothing, and household goods and put Mike to work helping her move stuff from place to place. We sent some items to the thrift shop for sale, donated a few others, and packed our personal goods. When I wasn't studying for my early finals, I inventoried things we were having shipped.

The train ride to and from school became my study hall. Instead of playing cards with my friends—the three boys—I sat alone reading and memorizing. My final grade in German particularly concerned me. We had been reading Goethe's *Faust—auf Deutch—*and without an English translation. I had no idea what the book was about.

Luckily, that teacher didn't require a final.

After taking my exams early and preparing for the move, I thought about my future.

Several weeks before Dad's announcement about his transfer, I had received two letters—one from each of the colleges to which I had applied.

Dear Ms. Greene:

The admissions committee has carefully reviewed your application for admission to our school. Regretfully, we cannot offer you admission at this time.

Talk at school centered around the prom and graduation. We discussed our plans as hopes and dreams. After all, what could we do in a foreign land? Marrying and having children occupied our idle talk. So, when these letters arrived, I simply resigned myself to another disappointment.

Dad didn't. He spoke with one of the lieutenants who worked with him and arranged a meeting with me. The lieutenant talked about his alma mater and the fact that his mother was the dean of women there. His wife's father worked in admissions at the same institution.

"Fill out this application, write an essay, and I'll send it to my mother and see what they can do for you," he told me.

I had not heard from that particular school until one evening after Dad came home from work before our scheduled move.

"Do you remember, Peggy, speaking with one of my lieutenants about the possibility of your attending a school in upstate New York?"

I nodded and looked up at Dad's dancing brown eyes. I had completed the application and written the required essay but doubted my acceptance. He handed me an official-looking envelope.

I read the letter silently then looked up at my dad. "I've been accepted. I'm going to school in New York." I wanted to jump up and grab Dad and hug him.

Instead, I read the letter aloud to be sure I understood. The college accepted me for the semester beginning in September. "There is a provision, though. I'll need to retake the SAT and pass it with a higher score."

"It's a private college," Dad said. "We will pay your stay for one year, but then you'll need to reapply for a less expensive school."

My elation at having been accepted waned as Dad placed more restrictions on my life.

Again, I have no choice, but I'm going to college and away from home.

I looked down at the long list of required summer reading enclosed with the acceptance letter.

Oh, boy. I'd better get busy. Who is this Plato guy anyway?

FIFTEEN

Stateside Again

Fort Polk, Louisiana, and New York (1965)

My family and I flew in commercial economy seats back to the continental United States in late April. Dad rented an automobile, and we drove into Brooklyn, where we stayed with his parents a short time—because fish and company go bad after three days. While there, we attended the New York World's Fair. Then, we visited relatives in New York, Chicago, and Pennsylvania on our way to our new post, Fort Polk, Louisiana. Seeing our relatives after our three-year absence, talking about our European excursions, and hearing their experiences helped alleviate my senior year's disappointments.

The trip from Chicago to Fort Polk became monotonous and tiring.

We arrived at Fort Polk in late May and stayed a few days in the transient officers quarters. Then, we moved into a small home in military housing just outside Leesville. For about a week, while waiting for our household goods to join us, we tossed and turned in sleeping bags on the floor.

During the days, Mother and I cleaned the already pristine house and lined all shelves in the kitchen with contact paper. "We don't want to start our life here in someone else's dust," she said.

I don't want to start my life here at all.

Louisiana was hot, muggy, and often wet. The land smelled like a swamp with thick underbrush, wetlands, and probably snakes and alligators—not to mention cockroaches and biting flies. However, Dad purchased a new station wagon and took me to obtain my Louisiana driver's license, so I enjoyed an occasional semblance of freedom as I took the car to Fort Polk.

I drove myself to the post library for books required as summer reading and to the commissary, post exchange, or snack bar—but only during daylight hours. Just before dusk three times a week, Dad drove me to the education center where I enrolled in my first class for college credit, Government 101. Dad waited around to take me home.

"I can drive myself to class and back. I know the way."

"Yes, I know. But it gets dark out here at night."

"I need to learn to drive in the dark," I said. "Let me drive home."

Dad gave me the keys.

I turned on the lights, clicked them from bright to dim, drove the speed limit, used my turn signal, and stayed on my side of the road. After thirty minutes, we arrived safely at home. I thought I had done a good job, but he still refused to allow me to drive alone in the dark.

"There are no lights. If something happens, you may have a problem," he told me. "I will continue to drive you."

After about two weeks, one of my fellow students, a sergeant, introduced himself to my father. "Sir," he said, "I'd be happy to drive Peggy home after class."

Dad laughed.

The following week, however, Mother needed the car. So, after dropping me off at class, Dad permitted the sergeant to drive me home—within a twenty-minute window. After several more drives, the sergeant asked me for a date. I agreed, but I was still a little girl and not quite ready for sergeants. Our date, although friendly, ended a little scary.

Dad gave me the car keys, and I learned to drive after dark.

While I'd studied government principles in my college course that summer, outside of class, I also learned about what our government was putting into practice. I had not heard much about the war in Vietnam while living in Germany. The novel experience of watching multiple American television channels at Fort Polk showed graphic details of the fight we were supposed to be winning. Increasing numbers of young men drafted into service showed up for training at Fort Polk. Dad became the commander of Company D, 2nd Battalion, 4th Training Division.

Meanwhile, I prepared for going away to college in upstate New York.

Mother and Dad presented me with three sky blue Samsonite suitcases: one large, one medium, and one small, an overnight bag. My initials, *MG*, embossed in gold on the sides, and the new leather identification tags fastened on each handle gave me a slight sense of foreboding. *I'm going away.*

In truth, the fear didn't last long. I couldn't wait to leave. Ready to conquer the world of academia and finally make my own choices, I wanted to jump up and down and clap.

Before I left, I had to pack, and that meant deciding what to take and what to leave behind. The first items gave me no trouble. Into the open suitcase on my bed went Koala and Raggedy Anne. Next, I tossed in enough underclothes for seven days—my panties had the days of the week embroidered on them. My lovely prom dress needed to come with me as well as a beautiful cocktail dress Mother had stored in her closet. As she said, "I understand they have dances at this school."

Ooh, I wanna go.

Of course, I would need my coat, gloves, a sweater, and a hat. I didn't have any boots, but I packed an extra pair each of flats, high heels, and tennis shoes. Beside the suitcase, I laid out my slacks, a couple of pairs of shorts, blouses, and several skirts and dresses. And two pairs of pajamas—one baby doll and the other flannel with long sleeves. The stack on my bed looked like a mountain.

How am I gonna get all this into two suitcases?

I didn't.

Mother helped me pack. She handed me one of Dad's long suit-hanging bags for the dresses and heels. Then, she found a cardboard box for my stuffed animals and my other shoes, and she shipped it to her mother, my Grandma Mabel. I looked forward to staying with her in Peekskill before the semester began in late September.

"Remember," Dad said, "Grandma Mabel will worry until she hears from you, so call her as soon as you land. My father will meet you at the gate. You'll stay with Grandpa Patrick and Grandma Margaret in Greenpoint for three days, and then Grandpa will take you to the bus station. You'll purchase your ticket to Peekskill. Do not get off that bus until you reach the Greyhound Station. Grandma Mabel will meet you there."

I checked my luggage at the Trans World Airlines counter and carried my coat in my arm. Excited yet wary as to what the future might bring, my first solo flight ended three hours later at the newly renamed John F. Kennedy International Airport in New York City. I walked toward a long row of black pay phones along the wall.

I've seen people use these before. How hard can it be?

I picked up a receiver and dialed Grandma Mabel's number. Nothing happened.

"Excuse me, sir," I said to a man walking by.

He stopped. "What can I do for you?"

"How do I use this telephone? I don't know what to do."

The gentleman smiled. "Pick up the receiver and put a dime in the slot. Then, dial your number. The operator will tell you how much money it will cost to place your call. Do you need any change?"

"No, thank you."

He walked on.

Oh, my. There are things I need to learn in this country. Feeling a bit chagrined, I picked up the receiver once again, stuck a dime in the slot, and dialed the number.

A voice said, "Deposit fifteen cents." I did.

A few minutes after I spoke with Grandma Mabel, Grandpa Patrick walked up beside me. An old-school man of superior intelligence, my father's father always seemed austere and a bit formal. His head of thick, pure-white hair, his impeccable attire, and his posture gave him an aloofness that falsely indicated he was unapproachable. I loved and respected my Grandpa Patrick, but I would never confide in him.

My grandfather guided me through the terminal, carried my luggage, and hailed a cab—my first taxi ride in the United States. As we settled in the backseat, the driver clicked the meter. I watched, leaning forward and gripping the back of his seat as we stopped and started in the most populous city in the United States. My neck pivoted from side to side and craned up and down as I gaped at the skyscrapers and marveled at the crowds of people hurrying across streets. Horns honked, now and then something banged into something else, and fog or smoke or exhaust settled everywhere. I loved every minute of watching this living, bustling city.

Grandpa paid the taxi driver and tipped him a couple of extra dollars. "Always have enough change to give a tip," Grandpa said, "and never walk anywhere alone."

Grandma Margaret, who did walk everywhere—and usually alone—greeted me upstairs in their familiar railroad-style apartment with its two windows and a fire escape. The bathroom still had a cast-iron, lion claw-foot tub, and a pull-string dangled from a single, sixty-watt incandescent light bulb. I settled on the huge, well-worn, comfortable bed in which the three brothers—my father, Uncle Pat, and Uncle Jimmy—had slept. On the iron headboard hung Grandma Margaret's pearl rosary. Their four rooms felt like home.

That evening, I relaxed for a while in Grandpa's chair by the back window, watching the light atop the Empire State Building, then the tallest building in the world, go around and around.

The next day, Grandma and Grandpa and I walked to the subway and rode the underground train out to Flushing Meadows Park in Queens. This was not my first time in the subway, but even the turnstiles seemed as daunting as the smell. *I'm glad I'm not alone down here. I'd get lost. There's no way I could navigate this city alone. How would I get up from those tracks if I fell?* Realizing that I would someday have to do this by myself scared me.

Even though I had visited the 1964–1965 fair three months earlier with my parents and brother on our way from Germany to Fort Polk, I felt just as excited this time with Grandma and Grandpa. He wore a full suit, and Grandma wore her dark dress with a wrap. I wore long pants and a sweater. By the time we joined the crowd at the gigantic metal world globe called the Unisphere, we were already winded, and my feet hurt. But we soldiered on through the Carousel of Progress and the General Motors Futurama. We viewed a giant replica of Michelangelo's *Pietà* and the World's Largest Cheese from Wisconsin. I relished my first taste of a Belgian waffle, complete with strawberries and whipped cream. *Yum.*

Grandpa Patrick escorted me to the Greyhound station, purchased my ticket, and waited beside me. With bags and boxes loaded under the bus, I climbed the steps, handed my ticket to the driver, and chose a seat midway back and next to a window.

I was on my first unaccompanied bus ride across the wilds of New York State through White Plains into Peekskill. *This is so exciting. Every day will be a new adventure, and now I can do whatever I want. No more rules—just me and college.*

College.

Wow!

SIXTEEN

Return to Family

New York (1965)

Grandma Mabel Purdy met me at the bus station in what seemed like the middle of nowhere. I knew the stop. Our family had passed there many times on visits over the years. We started talking simultaneously, excited as puppies needing to pee, neither of us hearing the other.

Over the years, my mother's mother and I had developed a special relationship. Grandma Mabel and I always discussed everything, even stuff neither she nor I would share with anyone else. On our way to her house, she dished out all the family news about my cousins. I told her about my various firsts in New York City—riding the airplane alone, seeing the World's Fair twice—and the differences I saw between life in Germany and the United States.

After arriving at her four-room, one-bath home, we sat in the kitchen giggling as if we were both teenage girls. Grandma laughed from her belly, and her eyes teared. Then, she inhaled, sucked her teeth, and said, "Oh, my. Look at the time."

We scrambled ourselves into her four-door, secondhand Plymouth Valiant. I rolled the window handle around and around to lower the glass for a breeze. Grandma drove us to Valeria Home, a once exclusive resort now nursing facility, where Grandpa Sydney Purdy worked as the top mechanic.

This place looks like a castle or perhaps a fortress. It sure is old.
All my life, I had known that Grandpa Syd worked at Valeria Home. Often, as a child, when I visited my grandparents in Peekskill, Grandma woke me early in the morning. We pulled bathrobes on over our pajamas, slid our feet into fuzzy slippers, and drove through the woods over narrow, gravel roads to pick Grandpa up from his night job there. The only person who knew how to keep the antiquated furnace working, Grandpa had become indispensable.

Grandpa's face appeared cracked as his tired smile emerged. "Good to see you, Puggy," he said, calling me the name Uncle Robert attributed to my pug nose when I was tiny. Grandma scooted over—the car had no seat belts to get in her way—and Grandpa drove us home.

Once inside the house, he dropped his empty, black lunch pail onto the table, scrubbed his hands at the kitchen sink, and walked into the living room. Grandpa sank into his old but comfortable brown-and-rust-colored overstuffed chair and switched the television to a sports show. He remained there every night until Grandma called him for dinner. After eating, he did the same.

Around nine p.m.—or after the last wrestling match or baseball game—Grandpa released a deep sigh, stood, and stretched.

Then, he said, "Good night," and walked into his bedroom while still chewing bubble gum. As a baseball player in his high school days, "Slugger" Purdy had stuck Wrigley's Spearmint into his mouth, chewed throughout the games, and spit the chewed gunk onto the field. In his later years, he switched to pink Bazooka bubble gum. Often, we found his used gum stuck on the bedpost in the morning.

While in the kitchen with Grandma each evening, helping prepare a casserole and a small, leafy salad to serve for dinner with a can of fruit, I confounded her by telling her how Mother cooked on a coal stove in Germany. I described the various foods I had tasted for the first time over there—sauerbraten, spätzle, *Kartoffelsalat*, *Knödel*, *Apfelkuchen*, and especially *Stollen*.

"Oh, my," she said. "You even sound German. Can you speak the language?"

"Ja. Ein wenig. Aber ich verstehen nicht viel," I said. Then I translated for her. "Yes. A little. But I don't understand much."

Whenever I visited Grandma and Grandpa Purdy, I slept on a cot between her bed and the closet, and we talked into the wee hours. She told me about her childhood, her silly dreams, and the latest gossip among her friends and people I didn't know in her neighborhood. We even laughed over imagined romantic flings.

One evening, however, our bedtime chatter took a different tone. Grandma opened up about the most unpleasant and traumatic day of her life.

"My brother, Burt, was still a baby," she started off. "I was probably six or seven years old or so. Before that day, Mama brushed my hair every night and sang us to sleep. She doted on us."

I remembered seeing pictures of my great-grandmother, Julia Irene Secor. Her photographs showed a pretty, petite, proper woman gazing lovingly at her children.

"My father told us we were going for a buggy ride into the country," Grandma said. "Mama wore a big, round hat and carried the baby. My sister and I sat in the back with Aunt Gertrude while Daddy handled the reins. After a while, we turned into a small, dirt path that led to a big, white building. Daddy stopped just outside the open gate where two huge men in white jackets waited.

"'Go with these gentlemen, Julia Irene,' he told my mother.

"'No, Allen,' my mother said. She held tight to the baby and refused to move.

"The men pulled her off the wagon, handed the baby to Aunt Gertrude, and dragged Mama through the gate toward the sanitarium. I recall her screaming and looking back at us as we turned and rode away."

After a silence, I asked, "Why did your mother go into the sanitarium? Was she nuts?"

"My sister did some research after our mother died," Grandma further explained. "Women had no rights back in those days. In the early 1900s, when a man wanted to rid himself of his wife without the stigma of divorce, all he had to do was sign her into a special home."

Grandma's sister, my great-aunt Evelyn, uncovered stories that Julia Irene often yelled at her husband, Allen Burtis Secor Sr. As a matter of fact, she threw a butcher knife at him. The blade missed. But Grandma said she remembered seeing the knife sticking out of the wood by the door when her father left.

Evidently, Grandma's father, a traveling salesman for Watkins Elixir, flirted with the womenfolk. "He was a ladies' man," Grandma used to say. "I think Aunt Gertrude had a thing for him. That's why she didn't marry until late in life."

As elements of the story unfolded over the years, I discovered this was only one of many quiet scandals kept alive by retelling and embellishment. Grandma and I giggled together while referring to other family tales as real-life soap operas.

I had often spent time with my great-great-aunt Gertrude, one of my favorite old folks. In her cluttered, three-story, colonial house on the hill beside the Boys Academy, I'd sit beside Grandma Mabel's aunt, listening to her stories while marveling at all the wonderful antiques crowded under stacks of paper. An intelligent, educated woman born in the late 1800s, she instilled in me a love of family history, genealogy, and acrostic poetry.

Our ride to the state-run old folks' home seemed unusually quiet, and I grew apprehensive as we parked outside the shabby facility. *If it's this bad on the outside, what's it going to be like on the inside?*

Grandma became agitated. "Peggy," she said, "I'm worried about what you'll think. Aunt Gertrude isn't the same as you remember."

We unlatched a small gate, stepped up a few stairs, and lingered a number of seconds on the porch before ringing the bell. The front door opened, and we approached a small desk inside a dimly lit parlor.

Immediately, the musty smell of old people overwhelmed me.

This is not right. Doesn't anybody clean anything? Open a window. Turn on a fan. It's hot in here.

I waited while Grandma spoke with an attendant who said, "She's in the great room waiting for dinner."

I looked about but said nothing. Many elderly people swayed to music only they heard. One cradled a doll. Another pushed a stuffed animal bundled under baby blankets in a doll carriage. Others wandered from corner to corner, aimless, mumbling the entire time.

Along with the dusty smell, the low-level din of movement and muttering added to the gloom.

"Oh, honey, have you come to take me home?" The woman spoke quietly as I passed. Her withered hand reached out to me. I stopped, took her hand in mine, squatted beside her chair, and looked into her sad eyes.

"How are you?" I smiled. "It's so good to see you."

I like old people.

I held her hand for a second or two before catching up with Grandma. She had made a beeline directly to the center of the great room.

Oh my gosh. That can't be Aunt Gertrude. She's so withered and small.

My beloved great-great-aunt had been squished into an oversized baby's high chair. Other wizened ladies were confined in similar situations. One sat cross-legged inside a playpen.

This is criminal. Don't cry. Don't get angry. I dug my fingers into my palms as I shook. My eyes blurred with tears. *Concentrate. Smile. Love.*

Grandma spoke to her mother's sister and then turned to me, reaching out her right arm as an embrace that pulled me closer.

"Aunt Gertrude," I said, bending down to her eye level. "It's Peggy. I've come to visit you all the way from Germany."

It took a few minutes for her to recognize me and understand what I said. Then, her eyes sparkled. "Yes. Yes." Her strong, bony fingers grasped around mine. "Yes. I've been writing for you. See?"

She showed me a small notebook full of her tiny, Spencerian, fancy cursive. Her lovely handwriting—full of flourishes, underlines, and swirls—had always intrigued me. It now had become illegible.

"That's wonderful." I smiled.

A woman dressed in white delivered a batch of colored fabric containing a variety of fibers and textures. Distracted, Aunt Gertrude picked up a swatch of material, fingered it, and lapsed back into whatever world her mind lived inside.

I shut down while Grandma fingered the cloth with her aunt. *We need to go. I don't want to see any more of this.*

Then, a woman dressed in a blue uniform swept the fabric from the high chair onto the floor. She placed a tray of mush in front of my great-great-aunt, who plunged her fingers into the porridge and scooped it into her mouth.

We can't even help. There is no spoon.

Grandma tried to guide the handful for her aunt. However, the aged woman shook and put up a struggle as if fearful of us stealing her food.

"Let her eat," someone said, so we left.

My grandmother and I spoke not a word on our ride back home.

I couldn't sleep that night. I ruminated on the couch in the living room, thinking and writing a poem about that visit and my great-great-aunt Gertrude. The conditions under which she spent her last days appalled me. The poem is missing, but the dominant thought remains.

I will never allow anyone else I love to suffer such conditions.

And I haven't.

As deplorable as I found the surroundings while seeing my beloved aunt, I later thought of that visit as a gift. Aunt Gertrude passed away in October 1965 while I was at school. Every day, I wear her wedding and engagement rings as my own.

SEVENTEEN

College Life

Alfred University, New York (1965–1966)

After visiting with Grandma Mabel in Peekskill and enjoying a lovely eighteenth birthday party with Kathy, my friend from our freshman year of high school, I set off for college. Grandma drove me—and my luggage—through the forests and foothills of the Allegheny Mountains.

Alfred University, a small private college in upstate New York, reminded me of the years my family lived at Fort Devens in Massachusetts. Fresh country air breezed through evergreen or deciduous trees along the sides of small hills where clear water ran through creeks over smooth rocks. Sidewalks and paths wound beside streams throughout the area. After a snowfall, the water turned to ice crystals but melted right away. Little mud remained after rain; gardeners kept the grounds green.

We entered the parking lot behind the freshman girls' dorm called The Brick, where mothers and fathers unloaded cars alongside their daughters. Fellas wearing purple jackets and broad smiles greeted us. The purple-jacket guys carried my suitcases, bags, and boxes right into my dorm room on the second floor.

"Isn't that nice?" Grandma asked.

Oh, yes.

As soon as I entered my dormitory room, I noticed both the top and bottom bunks already made up. Each had stuffed animals sitting on the pillows, so I dumped my belongings onto the single mattress by the door. One window allowed light into the room. Three small, four-drawer desks, each with a chair pushed in, completed the furnishings. A huge walk-in closet with built-in drawers served as a dresser with ample space for three women's clothing. A slanted shoe rack held footwear.

During the summer, I had corresponded with my two roommates— Jackie and Pam. I wondered which had strung a large fishnet from the ceiling. The net dragged across the wall and held varied stuffed animals.

Before long, I too settled in. A lamp, a monthly calendar, and a soup can I had decorated in Louisiana—filled with a zoo full of sharpened pencils—went on my desk. I nailed an official university bulletin board above it. Raggedy Ann and Koala Bear lay comfortably across my pillow.

Each dormitory room in The Brick—built only for freshman girls—appeared identical. Large restrooms at one end of each hall contained a row of sinks with mirrors along an outside wall, a communal shower with four faucets, and several toilets between stalls. The bathroom reminded me of the dormitory at Nürnberg American High School.

After walking with Grandma for a while, since she had never seen a college campus before, we hugged. "I'll send you care packages every now and then," she said. I waved as her car drove off.

Feeling giddy and finally on my own, I returned to my room to unpack.

Before classes began, I attended a welcome orientation with all the other freshmen. As I milled about studying the map of the campus, picked up papers, and introduced myself to a group of professors, a diminutive woman asked my name and then introduced herself. "Hello, Margaret. I'm the dean of women here at Alfred. I hoped I'd meet you. My son was in Germany and wrote about you when you sent in your application," she told me.

"Yes, ma'am." *Okay, I wonder what he said.*

I had known the lieutenant with whom Dad spoke was the son of an administrator at Alfred University and that he had married the daughter of some dean there, but I hadn't fully thought through the implications until then. *I should have figured out I didn't get into this school on my grades alone.* Even though I graduated with a high B average and was on the honor roll, my SAT score had been just shy of the entrance requirements.

"I'm happy to be here, ma'am."

Now, what do I do?

"This punch is delicious. Why don't you try some?" The dean pointed me in the direction of the refreshment table.

Saved. I'll get some punch and cookies and be on my way. I placed all the brochures and pamphlets I'd gathered into a purple-and-gold cloth bag, grabbed a frosh beanie, and escaped back to The Brick.

For the first two weeks at Alfred, we freshmen wore our purple beanie frosh caps. That way, upperclassmen knew they could pick on us. I saw this hazing as part of the entire college experience. During those two weeks, I heard rumors that upperclassmen—fraternity brothers—made freshman boys wear skirts to class and drink water until they puked, but I saw none of that.

One day, while walking from the student union to The Brick, a male junior stopped me and said, "Carry my briefcase and walk with me back to my fraternity house." He set the case on the sidewalk and continued walking without saying anything else. So, I picked it up and followed, hoping he'd slow down and talk.

Instead, he saw another co-ed wearing a beanie and stopped her. He told her to skip beside me as I carried his briefcase. She did! Her name was Kathy—just like my cousin's and my high school girlfriend's in Peekskill—a good sign. We both laughed and took turns carrying the briefcase to the guy's fraternity house all the way at the far end of campus and up a hill. By the time we reached the house, the three of us skipped and laughed together. He asked me for a date to the fraternity's first house party, and Kathy and I became friends.

On another day, while Kathy and I walked on campus wearing our beanies, two men attacked from behind a tree. We screamed. They guffawed and fell in beside us.

"What do you think we should do with these frosh?" one said to the other.

"Take them to our house," the other said.

"Sounds good. What for?"

"They can clean the bar." The first one showed a coy smile on his face.

"Follow us, girls. We need scrub people to clean our bar before the big party."

The big party? Maybe we'll get to go to the Big Party.

When we arrived at the frat house, the guys led us into their filthy basement. The bar—covered in stale liquids of indistinguishable sorts—and the floor—full of cigarette butts—needed more work than mere refreshing. They handed us a boom, a large garbage can, and a pile of rags. "Get to it, girls."

Kathy and I worked for about an hour before the frat boys returned. "Here." One handed me a small piece of paper with the house address. "Come back tomorrow to finish what you've started. Then you can rake the leaves in the front."

I don't think so.

I felt hot and tired and unhappy. On our way back to The Brick, Kathy and I discussed our dilemma. "What do you suppose will happen if we don't return?" Kathy asked.

"I don't know. They can't kick us out of school. Can they?"

We chose not to return.

At the end of the week, our hall monitor—a junior who lived in The Brick and inspected our rooms daily—appeared at my door. She confiscated my beanie.

Oh no. She took my itty-bitty hat. Good riddance. I wonder if she took Kathy's. I looked down the hall and saw the monitor had taken my friend's beanie too. *Now what?*

Several weeks later, Kathy and I both received an ominous summons for frosh court. Fearful we would find ourselves in worse trouble if we skipped out, we arrived at court with what looked like at least a hundred other guilty-looking freshmen. Upperclassmen wearing black robes processed into the hushed hall. At the bailiff's instruction, we all raised our right hands and swore to tell the truth and nothing but the truth. Then, the bailiff called each of us to stand in a particular space while our crimes were read.

Talk about scary.

"Miss Greene," the court lawyer announced, "you have been charged with leaving the scene of a fraternity without completing your task. Is this true?"

Is this for real? I shook so much I struggled to say anything, but with effort I managed a single word. "Yes."

"What sayeth the court?" the fake lawyer asked the fake judge.

"For this offense, your beanie has been confiscated. And you will return to the fraternity at a later date to rake the leaves," the judge announced and pounded her gavel.

Huh?

No one smiled or laughed. This ceremony appeared legitimate and felt serious, but I had one thought: *I'm not going to rake any leaves.*

I didn't, and nothing more was said or done about it.

I felt grateful there were no other penalties imposed upon me. Taking a full load of academic classes meant spending lots of time studying at the library. Writing notes in shorthand while practically asleep and then transcribing them into English using my typewriter became my normal practice. Staying up all night—with the aid of NoDoz just before exams, which cropped up announced only on the beginning syllabus—led to short-term memory cramming rather than long-term learning.

College required more effort than I'd ever expended and, of course, more money than my parents had. So, rather than receive an inevitable D in biology while attempting to learn all about DNA and chemical changes, I dropped the class.

Although I passed the German qualifying exam and entered German 201, a sophomore class, I was ill prepared. The professor expected us to understand and speak *auf Deutsch*—in German. At one point, terribly frustrated with our class, he slammed his brief-case on his desk and stormed out. Shocked, we stayed in our seats for fifteen minutes before anyone dared leave. After some discussion, many students ditched the class, but I stayed. I wanted to get my foreign language credits over with as quickly as possible.

Unfortunately, one of the male students chose me as the object of his unwelcome teasing. After living overseas for so long, I was out of touch with American slang and felt unable to handle this unwanted attention, so I chose to tease him back. I used a German phrase spoken by our maid when we lived in Bamberg. She had called my brother "*lous poo*"—meaning little imp—and I pronounced the words with a negative tone.

This kept my nemesis confused for four class periods. Then, he grew smarter and asked our teacher what the words meant. Afterward, the boy asked me for a date. I declined.

Thus ended my attempt at teasing.

Our professor, thankfully, assigned no final exam or term paper. Instead, he gave us each a newspaper article written completely in German and told us to critique the article in English. My dog-eared German–English dictionary saw a lot of action. However, I forgot about the different grammar rules, so my paper made no sense. The professor must have taken pity on me; I received a C with a note written in German: *Du habst den Punkt verpasst. Es gibt kein Verständnis von Pronomen.* You have missed the point. There is no understanding of pronouns.

Unlike my decision to drop biology class because I'd received a D, I chose to accept my C in German 201. It was high enough that I would soon complete my language requirement.

During the summer prior to entry into Alfred University, I had taken a class on post about government and enjoyed it, so I thought about becoming a lawyer rather than the teacher I had always planned to become. One course I needed for graduation and would find useful in my chosen profession of law was Speech 101. *It wouldn't be bad for teaching either.*

On the first day, the professor asked us each to say the word *bag*. When I said "bag," the professor jumped up in excitement.

To the class, he said, "Listen to her speak. She has no accent. That's the way English should sound." Then he asked, "Where are you from, Miss Greene?"

"I'm an army brat," I said. "I don't know where I'm from."

Three weeks later, I had learned I had no problem speaking in a group, but giving a speech in front of a class full of uninterested people terrified me.

"Miss Greene, you're up," the professor said.

Shaking, at first, like boards in a hurricane, or maybe a tornado, I then froze. I couldn't rise from my chair.

"You can do it. We're all interested in what you have to say," he said.

I swallowed, took a deep breath, fingered my notes, and left them at my seat. One foot stepped in front of the other. I turned toward the class and saw all those bored faces staring at me. My voice quivered as I spoke:

This speech is about Santa Claus. He's coming soon, over Christmastime, but he's not the reason for Christmas. As a matter of fact, our Santa Claus really doesn't exist. His mythical origin is that he was Saint Nicholas, a real bishop, who came from somewhere near Turkey in the Middle East. But I don't know where that—

"Find it on the map," a tall upperclassman yelled. "I come from there."

Surprised—and scared—I grabbed my purse and fled out the door. I ran across the campus, into The Brick, and up the stairs. I didn't stop until I collapsed onto my bed—crying.

Later, after I spoke to the professor in his office, I was given a second chance. This time, there were no interruptions. I received a C, which was good enough for me.

Academically, I wasn't doing well. I had dropped biology, run out of speech class, and learned no German. I took no math class. I couldn't remember any civics—though English was part of civics— and I slid through government.

But I sure had fun.

In 1965, the legal drinking age in New York was eighteen— *yippee*—and fraternities everywhere were noted for their frequent drinking parties, but Allegany County was dry. A few miles away, however, Steuben County was not. Not surprisingly, all fraternities and most sororities in Alfred—situated on the border between Allegany and Steuben counties—served alcoholic beverages. Some students even learned to make their own moonshine, mostly wine and beer.

Every Saturday at Alfred, a frat party somewhere hosted dancing, drinking, and sometimes dangerous stunts. Mostly, the guys and gals at these fraternity parties looked out for each other, studied enough to pass or graduate, and looked forward to kicking back and having fun. That is where I met Chuck.

Chuck, a bit roly-poly, always smiled. He was the life of the party, danced well, and treated me like a lady. He and I attended many such events or drove around the area joining his fraternity brothers for a beer and pizza. We cheered at football games and sang along at university-sponsored concerts featuring contemporary artists like The Kingston Trio and The Four Seasons. On several occasions, we drove out of town, rushing back to beat the curfew.

Chuck was not my only beau.

I met Chip at a Reserve Officer Training Corps meet and greet I attended with Kathy at the start of the semester. Chip, good-looking, thin, and tall, smiled easily. His brown eyes always twinkled with mischief. Most mornings, Chip, either by accident or forethought, met me on the walk from The Brick to Alumni Hall.

All 200-plus freshmen sat for two hours three times a week in Alumni Hall, starting at eight a.m., listening to various professors lecture about civics, which was really world history, or about how civilization began. I don't remember a thing they taught us, but I still recall the large, drafty frame structure in which we sat. A twelve-foot pine weather vane in the shape of a quill stood in front of the building.

Each student had an assigned, numbered seat used to keep track of us. There was no interaction between student and teacher. Upperclassman monitors ensured the frosh rabble remained quiet, but we stayed almost silent anyway during the nightmare of listening and taking notes.

Neither Chip nor I had classes immediately after our dismissal from the lecture, so we met to walk, talk, and have coffee or Coke at the Union until our next class. One of our favorite walks entailed strolling among the autumn trees toward Steinheim Castle, which, we read, was originally built between 1876 and 1880 by a professor who wished to make a private residence that resembled the castles in Germany. Sometimes, Chip made up stories of a haunting there, but I simply enjoyed looking at the old, neglected building, mindful of the castles I loved in Germany.

Chip and I talked about all sorts of things. He had a sense of humor I didn't fully understand, but I enjoyed it anyway. We laughed a lot. He also sang in the ROTC men's choir.

Freshmen were not permitted their own transportation. Chip and I sometimes hitchhiked out of town to the edge of Steuben County, where most of the students drank, danced, and partied. One evening, a car slowed down, passed by, backed up, and returned to pick us up. When we climbed into the automobile, Chuck, with several of his fraternity brothers, laughed and drove us to the bar.

I felt mortified. Here I was dating one man but being picked up by another. *Burn a candle at both ends and get scorched.*

Downing more than one Jack Daniel's and Coke snookered me, but a *Löwenbräu* beer tasted refreshing. Drinking made me want to dance, but when I'd had too much, tears started flowing. Only now and then did I become a crying drunk.

Every dormitory, sorority, and fraternity had a housemother in addition to the floor monitors. One night, at exactly ten p.m., I entered the dorm a bit wobbly. I managed to reach the bottom of the stairs without falling, but making it up those steps seemed more daunting, so I clung to the railing and pulled.

Oh jeez. Everything spins. Don't feel tingly and fuzzy anymore. I need to sit down. I'll stay right here on this bottom step.

"Come on, Peggy. I'll help you up." My friend Kathy took my arm.

"Let her go," someone up above said. "She has to make it up the stairs on her own, or I'll have to report her."

Kathy stayed beside me as I pulled myself up the stairs, staggered into my room, and flopped onto the bed. Thankfully, the voice from above—my hall monitor—did not report me.

During this time in our culture, men outnumbered women at nearly every university as in the military. Unlike my peers growing up on posts, however, the guys at Alfred had no curfew. They never worried about time constraints.

We women, on the other hand, had to sign the official dorm roster at the time we left and when we returned. The Cinderella hour for freshmen girls was ten p.m. Sophomores and juniors signed in by eleven, and seniors had to return no later than midnight. As a dandelion child—a soldier's daughter—who'd already spent high school years in military dependents' dormitories, having a curfew felt normal for me. I had no problem adhering to these rules.

University rules also required a woman under the age of twenty-one to provide her parent's or guardian's written permission if she were to spend the night away from campus. Men left whenever they wanted. Another rule stated that unmarried students could not spend nights together at any hotels in the area. If a couple did, the woman was expelled—not the guy. If an unwed woman became pregnant, she was often ostracized, kicked out of school, or forced to marry. Women rarely reported rape or unwelcome advances.

These double standards between men and women, simply accepted at the time, lasted all the way through my college years. Talk about discrimination.

But since living by rules had always been part of my life as a child of the military, I didn't question these restrictions. Besides, where would I have gone? And with whom? At Alfred that year, most of the girls just wanted a husband, but I wanted a career and a husband. I got neither while there.

Immediately after hazing during Frosh Week, about a month after the start of classes, Greek Week began. I received invitations from all four sororities on campus.

I dressed in my blue cotton print swing skirt and my three-quarter-length-sleeved, turned-down-collar, blue print blouse. I carefully clipped my stockings to a garter belt and slipped on my black pump heels. While standing in front of the mirror with my roommates, I teased my thick, flipped-up blond hair. Pam and Jackie did the same behind me as I lightly powdered my nose and brushed bright red lipstick across my lips. Finally, I placed my dark-rimmed GI glasses on my face.

Looking good but not fancy.

I sighed and then bounced down The Brick stairs, out the door, and across campus to the various sorority houses.

After my first visit, I watched daily for a second invitation and received two: one from Sigma Chi Nu, the other from Theta Theta Chi. On the evening of the visit, I wore gray slacks with a striped beige pullover sweater, black pumps without stockings, and the same makeup, hairstyle, and eyewear. My roommates and I met up with Kathy on our way.

Theta Theta Chi sisters appeared friendly but seemed aloof to me. Sigma Chi Nu sisters smiled and joked. Several expressed interest in my experiences in Germany, but the atmosphere felt stuffy — not only outside.

A third invitation came from Theta Theta Chi but not Sigma Chi Nu. By this time, Pam and Jackie had become friends with the girls next door. They spent little time in our room except to sleep. I, on the other hand, spent time walking around campus with Chip — the guy I met at the ROTC dinner.

I had decided I wanted to join Sigma Chi Nu, not Theta Theta Chi. So, the last day of pledging, I donned my green shirt-sleeve dress — my best. I wore stockings and white heels, and I fixed my hair in a stunning topknot. Over my face, dolled up with makeup, of course, I wore my GI glasses.

The sorority meeting I crashed went well, or so I thought.

When I returned to the dorm, Jackie glared at me. Both she and Pam told me I should not have gone to the Sigma Chi Nu meeting without an invitation.

How did they know I had no invitation?

I received a summons to the pledge office in the administration building the next day.

Oh great. Another summons—just like frosh court. I keep getting into trouble without even knowing what I've done.

"Miss Greene," the receptionist in the office said, "we have received a complaint. You attended a party without an invitation. You have been blackballed for this year's pledge season. You may attempt to join as a sophomore next year."

Blackballed. What does that mean? Who complained? Why?

It didn't take long for my roommates to let me know they had been picked for Sigma Chi Nu. Jackie's sister already belonged. Further, they did not appreciate that I had attended their third meeting when I had not been invited.

It wasn't hard to surmise that my roommates had reported me, thus cementing an unease I had already felt around girlfriends.

I told myself it didn't matter.

The day before this humiliating meeting, the day of the unfortunate third sorority visit, I'd placed a phone call to my parents in Louisiana asking for money to join Sigma Chi Nu. Dad reminded me I would not be attending Alfred next year anyway. He, like most everyone else in the military, was preparing for his transfer to Vietnam. I needed to stay closer to home, which he said meant Fort Polk.

So, thus ended my quest for a sorority at Alfred.

In part, I consoled myself with anticipating a friend's upcoming visit. Kathy, the girl I knew from high school in New York—who happened to share the name of my present girlfriend at Alfred and with whom I had maintained a letter-writing friendship while in Germany—planned to come see me at school. Then, a week before Kathy's scheduled arrival, Grandma Mabel called. She informed me that my friend had died in a car accident.

How could this happen? Only old people die.

I had moved so often that I had not yet experienced the death of someone so young. I had no way of knowing I would too soon loose other young friends to death. In the meantime, I felt lost as I walked around campus listening to the chimes of the carillon. On Sundays, their notes melded with the various church bells in Alfred. After a while, these melodies faded into the background, as did my grief.

While the Vietnam War, hippies, flower people, demonstrations, drugs, and race riots crowded newspapers and television, I remained shielded in my naivete at Alfred University during the 1965–1966 school year.

Midway through, for Christmas vacation, I went home to Fort Polk, where my parents informed me—again—that I would not return to Alfred the following year. Our family had lived in Leesville for less than a year. I didn't want to live there, but once again, I had no choice. At that time, my father trained soldiers for combat. He expected his deployment orders within the next year or so.

After I returned to school from Christmas break, Chip presented me with a letter from his girlfriend in the city. I knew he had a high school girlfriend, but I had no idea they were as serious as indicated in the letter. She informed me that she loved him and—although being friendly was fine—I needed to realize he belonged to her. Chip and I remained friends, and we continued meeting for coffee and strolling up to Steinheim Castle on campus. He left Alfred at the end of the year, as did I.

Chip and I maintained a pen pal–relationship until 1968 when his girlfriend sent me another letter. I sobbed as I read this one. Chip had died from a drug overdose. Now, after losing a second close friend—and with soldiers my age going to Vietnam and with watching all the newsreels from that war—death became more real to me. It hurt.

Two years before receiving news of Chip's death and after Christmas vacation from Alfred in 1965, I grew more involved with Chuck, the fraternity boy I met earlier. Although Chuck left school for the second semester to work in Corning, New York, earning money toward his school expenses, he drove fifty-something miles every weekend to attend fraternity parties with me as his date. At the end of that semester, he gave me his fraternity letters in the form of a necklace. We had become *lavaliered*—fraternity-speak for going steady.

Still innocent when I arrived at Alfred University and living in a little girl's world, I wanted desperately to belong. After my attempted acceptance into a sorority left me blackballed and the frosh court confiscated my beanie, I searched for other means of approval. I decided the only place I belonged was within the military community.

Although I had never marched, at the end of the first semester, I initiated a freshman women's marching team with the support of the ROTC program. To my surprise, and that of the commander, twenty girls attended our first meeting. We met with cadet drill instructors twice each week at the gym. Seventeen of our original twenty practiced a choreographed routine in The Brick's basement. Simple maneuvers like *forward march, right face, to the rear,* and *column left march* became more complicated when we combined them with arm movements.

After about ten sessions, two of the ROTC cadets evaluated each of us. They chose four girls for their proper execution of marching commands. I ranked fifth.

Disappointed with my performance, I pouted.

Gee whiz. Real soldiers have six weeks of basic training every day before they have to present themselves for review. Of course, they learn a lot more than we needed to, but still.

The team gathered together and voted for a squad leader from among the four. We selected Tracy, a tall, thin, athletic woman as our leader. She had marched with a group in high school and knew her stuff. For our uniform, we chose a simple white button-down shirt-blouse with long sleeves and a straight-lined navy-blue skirt. We wore hose with white laced shoes, which were not of the tennis variety. With our leader chosen and our wardrobe in place, we prepared for our big debut in a local parade.

Many small groups on foot and some people with vintage automobiles, as well as a few floats, waited with us for their start. The Alfred University Women's Drill Team fell in behind the ROTC group.

The sun shone, but we felt the chilly air through our white cotton blouses. Shivering, yet in step, we marched. Moving as a group, each one of us nervous we'd forget or mess up the routine, we stopped at the parade stand. Tracy gave the command, and we stepped out. No one missed a beat. The crowd clapped. Giddy, feeling relieved and proud, we completed our routine without a misstep.

The next week, Tracy received an invitation for our team to attend the ROTC dinner at the mess hall on the men's side of campus. Excited, we sprayed our hair with Aqua Net, which acted like glue. We applied our makeup just right, donned freshly washed and ironed uniforms, and then leisurely strolled together across campus. Then, we entered the cafeteria.

Uniformed men—it seemed like hundreds of them—came to attention at exactly the same time.

What a sight.

Kathy and I glanced at each other. We couldn't stop smiling.

"Be seated," someone yelled. Chairs scraped. Everyone sat, and the voice spoke again. "It is my honor to present the latest addition to the ROTC program here at Alfred. Will the ladies of the Alfred University Women's Drill Team please stand?"

We stood. The entire room burst into applause. I looked for Chip but couldn't find him in the sea of uniforms.

We lined up first for our food, returned to our table, gabbed like the rest, slid our finished trays into the receptacle, and returned to our seats.

"Atten-hut." The boys stood again as we left the building.

Wow! This is great.

During the second semester, girls left the drill team, but others signed up. We numbered twenty-one, adjusted our routine, and continued practicing in the basement of The Brick. Toward the end of the school year, we were asked to participate in the ROTC matriculation ceremony.

Looking smart in our uniforms, we arrived at the parade grounds on campus. The place teemed with ROTC members already in the stands. Tracy gave the order, and we marched in step onto the field, took our positions, and then started our routine.

In anticipation, I began before I should have—the only member out of step—me! Tracy kept calling "left, right, left, right" while I continued going right, left, right, left.

Thankfully, our presentation only lasted a brief time—which, to me, seemed like forever. Finally, we returned to our seats in the stands to watch the official ROTC march onto the grounds. When their drill team presented its routine, fake rifles and all, Tracy yelled, "Atten-shun."

We stood on cue, but then Tracy started talking to someone and never released us to sit. One by one, we lowered ourselves when we got tired. I felt ill at ease.

We really are playing at this.

I spent much of my downtime practicing with the women's drill team. My parents had given permission for me to leave campus—particularly to visit with my grandparents in New York City. Most weekends, Chuck drove from Corning to Alfred when we attended his fraternity parties or spent time with friends off campus. Kathy, Chip, and I palled around. I also studied more and raised my grades somewhat.

After retaking the SAT, I applied for a transfer to Northwestern State College in Natchitoches, Louisiana. Before leaving at the close of the school year, the drill team held a going-away party for me— the first such party held in my honor from all the places I had been. *Finally, I found a group in which I belong. But not for long.*

My parents agreed I could visit for a weekend the following summer, so Kathy, Chuck, and I made plans for a reunion and his fraternity's end-of-the-year bash in 1967.

Meanwhile, Mother, Dad, and my brother helped pack the family car with all my paraphernalia. I left Alfred thinking I'd return and everything would be the same.

It was not to be.

Summer Lessons Learned

Fort Polk, Louisiana (1966–1969)

Beginning in the summer of 1966, between studying at Alfred University and attending Northwestern State—then a college, now a university—in Natchitoches, Louisiana, I worked with family services as a counselor at the Fort Polk Summer Children's Camp every weekday over six weeks each year. Paired with service members from the entertainment corps, co-ed college student dependents of military personnel received compensation for a full day escorting and playing with groups of younger dependents. My section consisted of ten children ages seven to ten. We played games, made various crafts, ran relays, and went swimming—all on post. The soldiers, not much older than we, often teased us, although they were quite attentive to the children.

The bus unloaded at the swimming pool. We changed and escorted the children to the edge of the water and watched as they jumped in, swam, or simply played. Unfortunately, I suffered from aquaphobia. So, despite my time living in Hawaii, I did not know how to swim. Feeling uncomfortable, I walked around the pool watching each of my charges and worrying.

What should I do if one of them struggles?

165

One afternoon, I followed one of my older, more advanced swimmers to the deep end of the pool.

"Get her," I heard just before hands pushed me.

Down I plunged, water over my head, deeper.

Panic.

No! Don't panic. Float. Need air—don't open my mouth.

I thrashed my way up, gasping. Flailing.

"She can't swim!"

Splash.

Two strong arms lifted me out of the pool. Someone wrapped a towel around me as I shook.

"We were having fun," one of the soldiers, probably my age, said. "I thought you could swim." Then, of all the nerve, he asked me for a date.

I declined.

However, I didn't lack for company. During the summers of 1966 and 1967, cadets from West Point spent six weeks at Fort Polk. We camp counselors were asked to escort them to various functions at the Officers Club.

Yes. Yes, I can do that.

We ladies, decked out in our finest dresses, heels, and white gloves, gathered in the O Club foyer and eyed the tall, uniformed cadets. They strode across the floor and, as if we'd all slipped back into junior high, asked for our hands and escorted us through the general's reception line. From there, we dated under the watchful eye of the honor code.

We provided transportation for these cadets to go to the Officers Club on Saturdays for the weekly happy hour dance, and occasionally we attended a movie with them—always in a group setting. I invited one such gentleman to a picnic on post where he drove us in my father's car. This cadet reciprocated by inviting me to a private dinner with a West Point graduate and his wife at their home. But all daydreams of developing any romance or long-term relationship evaporated by the end of the cadets' six-week stay.

Not so honorable was the two-week reservist I met one lunchtime at the Officers Club. Louisiana's drinking age in 1967 was eighteen, so after a giggly, uncomfortable evening at one of the many soldier bars in Leesville—and having drunk too much—we took a drive.

"Where are we going?"

"Just on post. I left something at the office. Then, I'll take you home."

Instead, he stopped the car under a copse of trees behind a bunch of dark barracks. The nighttime air chilled, and the darkness surrounded me.

He smiled.

"Please take me home."

"In a little bit," he said, inching closer in the front seat.

I opened the car door, jumped out, and looked around. *No one in sight.*

The reservist stood behind me. "I'm not going to do anything you don't want. No one will hear you if you scream, anyway."

You're kidding. I'm so frightened I couldn't scream.

Quicker than a rodeo roper, he picked me up, sat me on the hood of his car, and laughed. "Are you scared? Don't be. I'm just playing."

Suddenly, everything seemed funny. "Take me down," I stammered, then laughed.

His eyes became big and his smile crooked—as if a thought had just entered his mind. "Okay, how about if I tie you to that tree?"

What? He wouldn't dare.

He must have been a cowboy in his regular life. A rope appeared, and I found myself tied to a tree.

Then things got serious, all traces of amusement gone.

"Untie me. Take me home. You don't want to get into trouble for this."

"I guess not," he laughed. "My wife wouldn't like it either."

His wife? He isn't wearing a wedding ring.

That night as I tossed and turned in my bed at home, I understood that some men could be dangerous. Luckily, I rarely ran into any of them.

My innocence still intact, I began classes in Natchitoches, Louisiana, that fall. Every summer, however, I returned to Fort Polk.

I worked at the children's camp again during the summer of 1967. One of the sergeants who worked with family service entertainment asked me to audition for a part in the post play titled *Rhinoceros*. Not having attempted such an experience, I agreed. The play—a metaphor about resistance to conformity, particularly communist or socialist ideas—portrayed the masses transforming into rhinoceroses. I played an old lady who conformed easily.

The play was a flop. Having difficulty remembering my lines, I believed its closing was completely my fault.

Never again.

Just before classes began in September 1967, Dad received his orders for Vietnam. In preparation for his deployment, we took leave and drove to New York so he could see his parents.

Dad and Grandpa Patrick sat opposite each other at the round table in the kitchen. When Dad explained the army had ordered him to Vietnam, Grandpa argued. "You've been through too much. You've served your country. I'll call my connections in Washington and get you deferred."

I understood that Grandpa was referring to the fact that my father had been a POW during World War II and served in Korea, but what connections did my grandpa think he had after all these years?

"No, Pops," Dad said. "The United States Army has been good to us. It's time I paid it back."

Proud of my father for saying that to his father, I still wondered why Grandpa thought he could change Dad's assignment just like that. *There's no choice with orders.*

The next morning, my father escorted me by subway and bus to Grand Central Station. He had remembered and kept his promise made at the end of my freshman year to allow me to visit Alfred University and attend my then boyfriend Chuck's fraternity bash.

"Dad," I said as he handed me my train ticket, "what should I say if Chuck asks me to marry him?"

My father pulled me forward, looked directly into my eyes, and said, "Peggy, if you were really serious about him, you wouldn't have to ask." Then, he kissed me goodbye, and I rode on to the Alfred train depot where Chuck waited.

I shouldn't have been surprised that Chuck had met someone else that school year—as had I. We attended his fraternity bash but had little fun. I stayed with my friend Kathy, and we walked around campus together. Then, I left the old behind.

Summers, being only eight weeks long, seemed much longer—especially after Dad deployed to Vietnam. They meant a constant battle between my mother and me. Our relationship was strained to begin with. However, once Dad left, Mother seemed afloat without an anchor. My brother, still a bit hyper, required a lot of attention, and I was away most of the time.

To top all that, I had a brief liaison with a lieutenant on his way to 'Nam after Dad's departure. "Peggy, how could you allow this?" Mother said when she discovered I was no longer virginal.

"Mom, I'm old enough to make my own decisions. Besides, it's no big deal."

"I'm sending you to the priest. You need to talk to him and figure out what you need to do. What will your father say?"

"I'm not pregnant."

"That's not the point. You've shamed yourself and your family."

"It's the sixties, Mother."

Even though I said these things, I thought I had made a big mistake. My strict family raised me with definite moral values, and I'd believed I needed to save myself for my husband. I had already learned in college from many of my dates that some men expected more than just talk and a movie. Sometimes things went a tad too far, and once that happened, there was no return.

I didn't want to become a bad girl. I was not going to be what the boys called *easy*, but I knew I was lost. Values I had believed all my life came undone, and I struggled with thinking I was no good.

Despite all my worrying, not only was I attending classes, studying, and dating but also working on campus for room and board.

The summer of 1968, with Dad still overseas, I elected to take a summer quarter on campus. Worn out, I returned home to Fort Polk after that semester for only two weeks before my senior year, but I became quite ill with a fever and a sore throat that wouldn't go away. My head pounded. My skin erupted in a soft, red rash. And I felt exhausted. *So tired.*

Dad's sister, my Aunt Kathleen, was visiting from Chicago when, after a few days of me lying around the house, my temperature spiked to 103°F. We rushed to the hospital, and the doctors made the diagnosis: mononucleosis.

For several weeks, I lay in bed feeling terrible. Classes started, but I could not get up, so I lost the first week or so of academic life during my senior year. Although, as Mother too often reminded me, many considered mono the kissing disease, my doctors told me the illness—caused by the common Epstein-Barr virus—was easily transmitted through the air by coughing. Miserable though I felt, I did recover and return to my college routine in my home away from home in Natchitoches.

Yet, Fort Polk remained home to me during the summers from 1967 through 1969. Although I worked for the summer camp on post at first, I later worked at the Officers Club as the party receptionist. I also would meet my husband there. But that's a story for the end of this book.

School, Dating, and Vietnam

Northwestern State College, Louisiana
(1967–1969)

In September 1967, I moved into the brand-new Sabine Dorm for women at Northwestern State College, now a university, and met my roommate, Linda Johnson. She was a tall, thin country girl who had a very definite religious bent. Many of our discussions centered around whether dancing and playing cards counted as sins.

On several occasions in her sleep, Linda sat straight up in bed, pointed her arm at a ninety-degree angle, and said, "Do you see the cross?"

I looked up and saw no cross but watched her arm fall beside her corpse-like body. A smile crept on her face.

This girl is weird. Even so, she and I became such good friends we roomed together during our entire college career—all three years.

Linda won medals for her singing with an all-girl quartet. I learned to harmonize while I sang along with her. She also studied hard and earned places on the honor roll and in an honor society. She and I sometimes studied together. I worked hard and managed to raise my dismal grades from AU to honor roll status of 3.5 GPA by graduation. During the last semester of our junior year, both Linda and I were invited to pledge the Phi Kappa Phi honor sorority, but when the time came for their choice, Linda was accepted. I was not.

Linda's major was home economics, and her goal was to find a good husband and live happily ever after as the best Pentecostal wife on earth. She later married Eric, a fellow she met at Louisiana State University in Baton Rouge, where she attained her master's degree, also in home economics. I've always hoped she had lots of kids and led the happy life she wanted.

When I entered college back in 1965, my goal was to become a lawyer. However, the academic troubles I had at Alfred—trying to remember facts in my government class and figure out DNA sequences in biology—convinced me to aim for a less strenuous profession. *But which one should I choose?*

Technology had not yet developed automated course selection, so registering for classes occurred in a large gymnasium where we stood in line for hours—only to find the course we wanted already filled. Then, we had to wait in another inching row. After shuffling my feet for several hot, sticky hours in these lines, I decided to find the shortest and sign up for whatever class it offered.

Thus I became an elementary education major. *Maybe I was meant to be a teacher all along.*

Coursework at NSC seemed less difficult and demanding than at Alfred University. Over the three years I studied in Louisiana, something called *new math* made its debut. As an elementary education major, that class was a godsend. Finally, after all my years in school, I understood why certain mathematical functions existed. Having to prove every step while performing division, for example, helped me understand the process. Fractions still caused some difficulty, but at least now I could explain why one-fourth equaled twenty-five percent. Square roots continued to confound me, but who in my third-grade classes would need to calculate the square root of something? Instead of worrying, I had fun with binary numbers, and now geometry made sense.

At the time, elementary education teachers taught every subject to the children assigned to their classrooms. My health and physical education professors had us play games like red rover, dodgeball, softball, and even heads up, seven up. Music education consisted of learning to play a tune on the xylophone and kazoo while sight-reading notes from the old-fashioned songbooks of the fifties.

But reading education became my favorite course.

The professor had taught in Louisiana's public schools for years. She presented us not only with the history and theories of reading for elementary school teachers but also with actual lesson plans and hands-on manipulatives for use when teaching children of all levels. She planted the seed of excitement for teaching children to read.

I want to become a reading teacher. After all, many children find reading difficult. Who can blame them when boring books like Dick and Jane *are still in use?*

Techniques for teaching children to read—reading games such as word relays, word walls, phonetic bingo, read-a-longs, and language news stories—piqued my interest. I poured through and scoured teaching magazines, and I cut out and created teacher idea notebooks to carry with me wherever I went after graduation—for use in my classrooms.

I found my niche. I became a teacher.

After moving as often as I had, cultivating lasting friendships was difficult but also one of the skills I longed to develop. So, even though my first attempt at joining a sorority at Alfred University had failed, I tried again at my new school.

My suite mate, Pat Smith, was a Sigma Kappa Sorority member. After visiting the different sorority houses during Greek Week, I decided I wanted to join Sigma Kappa, ΣK. All my visits had been polite and friendly, so I felt certain I'd get in.

Disappointment hit me when I looked inside my mailbox and found no invitation to the final sister/hopeful party—their annual Hawaiian night. Since one of the initiation rites for the last week before acceptance forbade possible pledges from speaking with the sorority's sisters unless they spoke first, I said nothing.

"Peggy," Pat said the next morning, "I expected to see you at the party last night."

"You did?" I responded. "I wasn't invited."

"But you were invited, or at least, you weren't blackballed during our meetings," Pat said.

"Gee, can I still come? I want to join Sigma Kappa."

"Sure. Let me find out what happened and get back to you."

I did attend other meetings and was accepted as a pledge of Sigma Kappa, but fate stepped in, and I made a hard decision.

As a pledge, I was not allowed to drink alcoholic beverages until initiation. I attended a fraternity party—where alcohol flowed freely—with a date well-known to my sorority sisters. I drank only Coca-Cola, but I had a wonderful time laughing and playing and enjoying myself without the benefit of booze.

One of the frat boys took my date and me onto the porch.

"You know she is not supposed to be drinking," the fraternity guy told my date.

"She's not," my date said.

The frat boy didn't believe my date, so I smiled and said, "I'm not drinking. I can have a good time without any alcohol. Besides, why do you care?"

"I don't," the frat boy said. "But your sisters here do."

The next day, one of the Sigma Kappa women approached me about the sorority's standards to uphold on campus. "All Sigma Kappa girls are good girls," she said. "We do not have bad reputations, so you need to watch yourself carefully."

Well, I got mad. I've always had an impulsive streak, and I had a difficult time accepting the fact that some people—especially girls—jumped to conclusions in judging other people. After thinking about it overnight, I pounded a scathing letter of resignation on my typewriter. It went something like this:

Dear Sigma Kappa,

I am disappointed in this so-called sisterhood. I feel that I have been judged unfairly and will not be part of such a group.

Peggy Greene

I regretted sending the note almost immediately.

One weekend at the end of spring in 1967, just before finals, I decided on a whim to leave school for a quick visit home. When I arrived at our house just off-post, I couldn't believe what I saw: My home was empty.

I returned to school that weekend without knowing the whereabouts of my parents and brother. I worried and tried to reach them but couldn't. I failed my general math final on Monday and confused the dates and times on my other exams.

I learned a conflict had developed between the builder and my parents. It dragged on and could not be settled, so my father and several other officers moved our furniture from the house to storage. Meanwhile, the newspaper reported: "Soldier going to Vietnam. Wife and children homeless at fault of builder."

Mom called me later that week—after finals—to say they had returned home when the builder settled out of court. As was normal for my family, they hadn't wanted to worry me, so they had chosen not to let me know what was going on.

During the early fall of 1967, my father joined other soldiers as they gathered at the small, military airfield on base at Fort Polk. Too soon, they would board airplanes for their next destination en route to Vietnam. The sun shone, and there were no clouds, but I felt a gray mist had enveloped my family. Being a military family meant we put our lives on the line for our country's and others' freedom. But the war in Vietnam had become divisive and unpopular.

Watching my father and other soldiers prepare to depart left a hole of worry filled by fear. I wanted to be brave, so I did not speak of my angst. Dad grabbed his duffle bag, threw it onto the small plane, and then turned and waved before mounting the steps. He looked at us through the window and smiled.

I glanced at my mother, who stood stoically, and my brother, hyped-up with energy. I needed to maintain a calm, strong presence for them.

I watched my father's plane fly into the sky.

Then I cried.

During the summer of 1967, a lieutenant who worked directly for my father before he left asked Dad if he could date me. The lieutenant escorted me to the Officers Club dance where we wore matching red cloth draped around our bathing suits and won first prize in the costume contest. He often came to the house for dinner. Then, we went to a movie, and he always returned me safely home.

After Dad left for Vietnam, however, the lieutenant's attention increased to the point that we ended up having a two-week affair before he shipped out for jungle training in preparation for fighting in Vietnam.

Dad told me later that if he had known about the affair and then met up with the man in Vietnam, he would have killed him.

The year Daddy served in Vietnam, 1967–1968, was the worst time of my life.

The beginning of my junior year passed in a fog. I developed terrible, horrendous headaches, and I was fainting again. The only way to stop my head from hurting was to pull my hair straight up and away from my head. Doctors said there was nothing wrong, but they gave me Darvon to control the pain and Valium to deal with stress.

Taking the prescriptions helped. I spent the entire semester at school ingesting these drugs lawfully prescribed by military doctors. After my father returned from the war, I slowly weaned myself from the combination, yet I kept the two handy and used them sparingly. However, I wouldn't become completely free of Valium until several years after my children's births.

But that semester, I experienced lots of stress.

Mother said she was so disappointed in my having become a "bad" girl in college that she would no longer provide money for my education. I immediately wrote to my father, who must have negated Mother's threat. I decided, however, to get a job, so I started working in the cafeteria to help pay tuition. My time was now divided between working, attending classes, and studying.

Meanwhile, my father served in Vietnam.

The biggest topic of conversation at my school in 1967 and 1968 surrounded the Vietnam War. Men returning from the Far East told horrific stories, and every night the television showed war pictures never seen or even imagined. Young men I dated either feared the draft and tried to avoid it or trained in the service while knowing they must go to Vietnam but might never come back.

Although we witnessed no demonstrations around the base or in the schools in Louisiana, we were well aware of the antiwar rallies. All across America, soldiers coming home were treated poorly. Gruesome photos of fighting telecasted into our living rooms each night coupled with pictures of peace demonstrations, and propaganda from Jane Fonda fueled discontent among the American population. Civilians turned against our soldiers, blaming them for atrocities and forgetting they were honorably following orders given by generals encumbered by changing ideas from civilian politicians. I was ashamed of my countrymen for not supporting our troops.

The Tet Offensive began. Recruiters swarmed the campus.

I decided, on a whim, to enlist.

I visited all the recruiters on campus, but the uniform and bearing of the United States Marines impressed me most, so I signed on the line. Someone escorted me upstairs at the student union then gave me an aptitude test and subjected me to an interview.

Unknown to me at the time, it happened that a junior named James signed on that same enlistment line a few days before I did. He told me later about what happened while I completed my test. Nearby, he stood talking with a recruiter and other guys. They laughed together about the girl who wanted to be a marine.

One said, "She must be a train wreck."

"No," the recruiter told them. "She's quite pretty."

Not believing him, they waited to see for themselves.

When I walked down the steps after taking the enlistment exam, I heard a hush, a drop from the noise made earlier. Unaware of the reason for the sudden silence, I handed my test to the recruiter and left for class.

James said they were all stunned, and he decided he must meet that girl who wanted to become a US Marine.

That evening, while I cleaned tables in the cafeteria, a fellow I knew yelled, "Hey, Peggy." Five guys sat at his table, their food half eaten. "Come over. Someone wants to meet you."

My acquaintance introduced his friend. James, stocky and a bit overweight, wore glasses with rims as black as his short hair. He also wore a white cast from shoulder to wrist.

"What happened?" I asked. "You run into a tree or something?"

James snickered. "You mean this?" He raised the cast. "A bull took after me."

His friends guffawed. "You should have seen that boy run."

"A bull? A real boy-cow?" My eyes opened wide.

More laughter.

"Yup," James said. "He was quietly grazing, so I walked up to him real slow, speaking low. Just as I reached to scratch between his horns, he lowered his head—"

Laughter again erupted from the table.

"James ran like a scared rabbit." The other boys flailed their arms in the air, clearly enjoying the tale of their friend's misadventure.

James blushed but chuckled along with them.

From then on, whenever I happened to work, James seemed to be in line for his food, and he often met me in the cafeteria after my work shift. He studied wildlife management and liked everything about the outdoors. James also hunted and told me his favorite thing was going into the woods alone for days at a time. We had nothing in common—other than the fact that we both joined the Marine Corps at the same time.

The next step of my enrollment, according to the recruiter, was to undergo a physical exam, and someone would administer my oath. I would then go to basic training that summer.

I had no idea what I was doing.

One weekend, at my home in Fort Polk, Louisiana, a female marine administered the Oath of Enlistment. Mother took a picture of me while my brother looked on. I felt proud and excited. As we talked, though, I wondered whether I could make it through basic training in the coming summer.

We sent the photo to my father in Tay Ninh, Vietnam. On his next cassette tape, Dad congratulated me, but he also asked, "Peggy, are you sure this is what you want to do?"

Meanwhile, I wore my US Marine pin with pride.

When I took my physical at the army hospital in Fort Polk, the doctor said, "You appear physically fit. However, the history you've given me may prevent your acceptance. I don't have to report all these past episodes. You seem fine right now, and your tests show nothing abnormal."

"I just want to know why I've had these symptoms," I said. "I've felt faint upon occasion most of my life, sometimes losing consciousness. I've been tested and told I don't have epilepsy. My headaches can be excruciating. My only relief comes when I do this." I grasped my hair in both hands to show him. "And Darvon helps."

The doctor sent his report but ordered no further testing.

During the rest of that semester, I lost consciousness once—right after receiving a cassette tape from my father.

The recording started with lighthearted talk and laughter. Suddenly, large booms and scratches like fast movement sounded.

Click.

Silence.

Dad's voice returned. "We just had a slight attack, but all is good here. Hope all is well there."

I shook, replayed Dad's tape, hid in the bathroom, and fainted.

The campus doctor prescribed Valium.

After several phone calls from a doctor in Washington, DC, I received a letter rejecting my enlistment. The US Marine Corps recruiter verbally suggested I enlist in the army since their qualifications were not as stringent.

Good. I don't want to go anyway.

During my 1968 summer semester, I earned money as a teaching assistant. One day, an older woman knocked on the door of my dorm room. "Hello," she said. "My name is Mrs. Stubid. I was told you could help me understand this thing they call new math."

"Certainly." *She must be at least fifty. She's ancient. Why would she need new math?*

For the rest of the semester, Mrs. Stubid came to my room, and we studied together—my first real teaching experience. She told me she had been teaching for many years in a backwoods, country school there in Louisiana, but a new edict came out that she needed to renew her teaching license. However, the new math thing had her stymied. Together, we slugged through the unfamiliar nomenclature for old concepts and proved every operation. I discovered a respect for both the old and the new methods during this, my first attempt at teaching.

One upperclassman invited me on several dates. We attended his fraternity parties and went to football games or simply drove around town—with gas costing twenty-five cents a gallon. We stopped to eat, chatted, and participated in make out sessions we called *submarine races*. Sometimes, we ate at a local barbecue restaurant. Other times, his fraternity brothers and their dates met us. I enjoyed being with him, but we both understood our relationship would not go any further than friendship.

With the war raging, most college men knew they would be drafted once they completed their studies, but this man didn't fear; he was happy. Some lawmaker had pushed a bill through Congress that exempted lone males from service. As the only male left of his family, he had received a number that excluded him from serving. Some men, without such an exemption, hightailed it to Canada—where no extradition treaty existed for draft dodgers—but most men of my acquaintance enlisted, attended basic training, and served their time honorably.

In the fall of 1968, this upperclassman invited me to the homecoming game in Shreveport, and I accepted. I made plans to stay at the dorm with some friends who studied nursing. He would meet me there, and we'd go together to the game.

The weekend before homecoming, he gave me a bottle of perfume. "I like all my girls to wear this," he said.

I should have realized I was headed for another shock that would rock my world for many years to come.

But about this time, a soldier I had dated the past summer called me. He hoped to be able to get leave to visit me before his deployment to Vietnam and asked me to break my homecoming date in case he could.

What else can I do?

I broke the date.

But the soldier never showed, so my roommate and I drove to Shreveport with friends, stayed in the nurses' dorm, and attended the game.

Several weeks after homecoming, the upperclassman called.

I wore the perfume all his girls wore, and he took me for barbecue. We drove around listening to the radio and laughing and then parked in a wooded area to watch the submarine races. We kissed awhile, and I apologized for breaking the date.

He mentioned he saw me there with my friends, but he had asked an old girlfriend to join him, so he had a good time anyway.

"Peggy," he said, looking at me from behind the steering wheel. "I select my women very carefully."

"Thank you, I think," I said and waited. *What is he talking about?*

Sitting with him in his car, as I had many times before, I had never felt threatened, but tonight was different. He bent over, crushing me on top of my chest, fumbling with my clothing.

I had been working hard on getting myself together, and I did not want to ruin it all with sex. "No. Take me back to the dorm," I said as panic built.

"I've picked you," he mumbled and pressed on.

I tried to push him away. I tried to open the car door, but he was too big. I felt dark, and dirty, like a used floor mat on which he, who had once been my friend, trod with muddy, slimy shoes. The force he used hurt me, but I was more shocked than angry.

"Thank you." He grinned and started the car. We drove to the dorm in silence. He dropped me off in front of the door. My mind swam in a sea of self-recrimination and doubt. *Have I just been raped? What should I do? Why did it happen? How can I face my mother, my father? What was different about this than the affair I had last summer? Why do I feel so awful?*

I couldn't face my roommate or even myself. All I wanted to do was run away like I had so many times as a child.

I slunk past the check-in desk in the dorm and right out the other side of the building. I escaped into the darkness of night, passing cars as boys parked and accompanied their dates to the door. I continued walking.

Just get away—far away.

A car door slammed, and a man's voice yelled, "Peggy!"

I ran.

"Peggy, stop. What's wrong?" James chased me until he caught me. He held me tight. I pushed him, but he held on, quietly saying, "Calm down, calm down."

We walked together. He listened as I told him about the evening and cried. Then we walked in silence until curfew.

I didn't report the incident because, like many, I decided it was my fault. Besides, going public would be humiliating; I'd be kicked out of school while that upperclassman would simply have his hand slapped. Although rape is a criminal act, few date rapes were prosecuted. I discovered later that only fourteen percent of the American population who'd been raped in 1967 filed a report.

I needed out of the dating scene. I had had enough. This trauma shamed me so deeply, I vowed never to tell my parents; it would take me ten years after my marriage to inform my husband.

As before, James waited for me after I finished work in the cafeteria. We took long walks together. We strolled around campus sharing each other's stories. We went to the movies or sat on a blanket in the same pasture where the bull had chased him—when it was penned. Together, we attended functions at the Catholic Newman Club. James and I enjoyed each other's company, shared many of the same opinions, and felt good together.

I felt clean again.

James asked me to marry him and purchased an engagement ring. When I wrote to my father, who was still in Vietnam, he sent a bar coaster printed with the words "Wait Out."

No bells rang when we kissed, and my toes didn't curl, but I felt warm, comfortable, and safe with James. By this time, I had dated enough boys and men to know I wanted a committed relationship.

Because James studied wildlife management, he dreamed of leaving for Africa to work on a safari. On most out-of-town dates, we explored zoos and talked about the various habits of animals we saw. As long as the creatures stayed behind bars, I was happy. We walked while holding hands, discussing our future in Kenya, where he would manage wildlife while I would work with the people.

Being young, we had no idea what we were talking about.

"The fall school semester ends in a few weeks. I'll be coming home for winter break," I told my mother over the phone. "When is Dad coming back?"

"Well, my friend is in your room. Her husband has orders for Vietnam, so I agreed to let her stay here for a while," Mother told me. "You'll need to be on the couch until we hear from your father."

What? I know this friend. She and her husband were stationed here with Mother and Daddy. Of course, her husband is going to Vietnam, but why isn't she staying in her quarters? What's going on?

A few days later, I hitched a ride from school to home and was greeted at the door by growling and yapping from Mother's friend's dog, a chow.

"I hope you don't mind," Mother's friend said. "I just couldn't stand being alone without my husband, so your mother graciously extended an invitation." Mom didn't smile or say anything. She just looked down at the floor.

"Isn't Dad coming home soon?" I asked.

"Oh, I won't be a bother," Mother's friend said.

"But you are," I said. "Haven't you and your husband been separated before? You know what life in the army is like. My dad is coming home from war. We need to be together as a family, alone." I dropped my bag on the floor beside the couch and stalked into the kitchen.

Mother followed me. "Peggy, my friend needs someone to help her through this. She is frightened."

"So are we."

Dad's return flight was scheduled for three weeks later.

The weekend of Dad's return, I hitched another ride with a friend from school to Fort Polk. Glad that Mother's friend and her dog had moved out, I hoped to see my father before returning to school for finals. However, a rainstorm closed in, and I had to leave with my ride before Dad arrived home.

Safely at school, I called home to check. I had to make certain Dad was truly there.

"I'm back, honey, all in one piece. Can't wait to see you."

Winter break began. The air felt dry, the temperature hovered around 75°F, and the Louisiana sky shone blue and sunny. I stepped off the bus coming home from college to see the beaming face of my father. He seemed thinner, but his smile was the same, and his hug felt as strong and welcome as ever.

Daddy's home. His tour in Vietnam is over.

We retrieved my suitcase from under the bus and walked toward the parking lot. Instead of Dad leading me to his blue Ford station wagon, we stopped beside a small, dusty red, 1965 Hillman.

"Merry Christmas, Peggy," he said. "It's yours."

This isn't what I envisioned for my first motor vehicle. Not this. I don't want a luxury car or a gilded Cinderella coach, but this jalopy has seen better days. I know I should be grateful and happy. After all, what college senior wouldn't want a paid-for automobile?

"Thank you," I said, looking in the side window while Dad opened the car's tiny trunk and set my suitcase inside.

Still smiling, Dad's brown eyes danced as he handed me the keys. "Get in. Start her up."

He settled into the passenger seat while I sat looking over the dashboard. "Dad, it's a stick shift. I can't drive this."

"Of course, you can. That is the clutch, the gas pedal, the brake. Step on the clutch, move the stick into first gear, step on the gas, and go."

Sure. This looks as easy as reading cursive when you've only learned to print.

I stepped on the clutch with my left foot, grabbed the stick with my right hand, moved it the way Dad told me, stepped on the gas with my right foot, and—*cough...scrape*—lurched.

We jerked forward. I stomped on the brake.

"It takes practice," Dad said. He tried to enlighten me on all the functions I needed in this machine, but I couldn't comprehend. He drove us home, explaining he would have loved to have had a car like this when he was my age. He had purchased it from a young captain he knew and thought I'd be thrilled.

I was not thrilled.

After discussions between both my parents and me, we decided to look for a not-too-new car with automatic transmission and air conditioning. Luckily, our neighbor happened to be friendly with a Chevy sales manager in Leesville who had a 1968 four-door sedan for sale. He gave my father a reasonable price, so Dad cosigned a loan.

I had my own top-of-the-line Chevy sedan—and a hefty bill to pay once I graduated.

The jalopy disappeared from our driveway, but I met the captain from whom Dad purchased the Hillman. Because this man was the same rank as my father and acted more mature than I, I decided he was older—maybe thirty.

He wasn't.

When the last semester of my senior year began, I left for student teaching in Shreveport, Louisiana. At the same time, James, whose grades were not good, reported to Parris Island for eight weeks of basic training. We set our wedding for the week after my graduation in May 1969. This dandelion child—a soldier's daughter—would become a marine's wife.

From Engagement to Marriage

Natchitoches, Shreveport, and Fort Polk, Louisiana (1969)

In January 1969, another co-ed and I applied and were accepted as the first Caucasian students from Northwestern State College in Natchitoches for integration into the segregated, all-Negro schools of Shreveport, Louisiana. We were the only white student teachers integrated into our all-black, inner-city school. I boarded in a Catholic women's home on the outskirts of downtown with two older women, so I relied on my Chevy Chevelle for transportation everywhere. I couldn't imagine what it would have been like had I accepted that old Hillman.

When I met my supervising teacher, Mrs. Hinckley, she asked, "What are your goals for teaching?" She sat behind a large wooden desk with a three-stacked box filled with papers to her right. A black vinyl grade book lay on the left. "Everyone who enters the field of education needs to have general goals and specific means to reach those goals. What are yours?"

"I want to become the best teacher possible," I told her.

Mrs. Hinckley smiled and said, "That will take some time and a lot of experience."

Twenty-one fourth-grade children entered the classroom, quietly took their assigned seats, placed their hands together on their desks, and waited for the start of their day. After opening announcements and roll call, Mrs. Hinckley said, "Class, I'd like to introduce Miss Stocker and Miss Greene. They will be your student teachers this semester."

My hands quivered. They felt wet and clammy. I wiped them on my skirt, faced the fourth-graders, and smiled. "My name is Miss Greene. I am happy to be here and look forward to working with you. I hope we have a fun time."

Breathing deeply, I sat and observed my first class in action. Mrs. Hinckley wrote instructions on the black slate chalkboard, distributed worksheets to two reading groups, and asked Miss Stocker and me to each sit with one of them while they worked. Mrs. Hinckley listened to a third group read in round-robin style before handing them worksheets too and moving to my group. She had the students correct their own papers. Then, she assigned the next lesson and called the class to order for arithmetic instruction.

Mrs. Hinckley, the only white teacher in the otherwise all-black, "separate but equal" Shreveport school, was a strong disciplinarian. With twenty years of classroom experience, she had mastered what she called "the teacher look," which could cow the most belligerent hooligans. If *the look* failed her, any student she sent to the office received immediate discipline and returned muttering apologies.

Being inexperienced in maintaining classroom order, I grew exasperated with one student during a math lesson. Sydney was bigger than the average fourth-grader, and his kinky hair looked gray from the dust he accumulated while wandering dark alleys at night. An angry young person, he appeared bottled up, ready to explode at any moment. When he came to school, his classmates knew to stay out of his way.

I didn't.

I completed a lesson on long division by walking around the room, helping students who appeared stumped. When I noticed Sydney fidgeting with something in his desk, I said, "Sydney, take your hands out of there, and give me whatever you are playing with."

"Why?" he muttered.

"You need to do your assignment. What is in your hands?"

"Nothing."

His paper looked blank. I peered into his desk, confiscated the Matchbox truck he had been playing with, and walked to the front of the room. "You may get your toy when your work is complete."

"Give that back!" he shouted. His chair hit the floor as he pushed his way out of his seat.

Stunned, I caught my breath just as Mrs. Hinckley took control. She escorted Sydney to the office, leaving Miss Stocker and me in charge.

I felt dazed, confused as to what had caused this child to become so irate. *I'm glad I didn't have to handle this situation alone. I need to make some sort of plan for if anything like this happens in the future.*

Once Sydney returned from the office, he said, "I'm sorry, Miss Greene."

"Sydney, what was so important about the Matchbox truck? And what caused you to explode as you did?"

"It was a gift from my big brother. He got arrested during a shoot-out at the grocery store last night."

I returned the toy, hugged the boy, and realized that children come to school loaded with their own problems.

Later, Mrs. Hinckley told me, "The first thing you must do as the teacher is make it known who is the boss. When that truth is tested, there must be consequences." The immediate consequence for Sydney was a trip to the office. After the child complied with the teacher order, an apology was expected. "Develop a *teacher look* and a stern voice," Mrs. Hinckley told me. Always know what you are going to do when challenged."

Mrs. Hinckley required Miss Stocker and me to write detailed lesson plans surrounding a unit on the human body. We collaborated in creating our unit encompassing the digestive, circulatory, and respiratory systems. Mrs. Hinckley allowed use of the textbooks but insisted we supplement the text with creative lessons.

Miss Stocker presented her lesson on the respiratory system first. She used posters and demonstrated how air enters and exits the lungs using balloons, water, a sponge, and a straw. My turn was next. *How can I top Miss Stocker's hands-on lesson?*

With no thought of the ramifications, I decided a simple demonstration dissecting a cow's heart would be interesting and different. *After all, a heart is a heart, whether it comes from a cow or a human.* The thought of blood didn't enter my mind. Neither did the age of my students. Or the memories of my first dissection, when I dashed out of my tenth-grade biology class—and fainted in the hall—right after our teacher handed me a gooey, slimy, wiggly sheep's eye to dissect. There had been no blood involved in that dissection.

So, after drawing and coloring posters showing the human heart depicting blue blood on the left side and red on the right, I called the local meat packing plant, ordered a cow's heart, and obtained sketchy driving instructions.

While procuring that heart, another incident occurred.

I hopped into my car without a map, turned on the ignition, and drove where I had never gone before—into the main city of Shreveport, Louisiana.

Forty minutes later, I steered into a gas station and asked for directions, but after following them, I could not find the appropriate street. I felt confused and tired.

My lesson is tomorrow. I've been driving around the same area for forty-five minutes and don't have a clue where this place is. It's got to be around here somewhere. I have to find it before it closes. What am I going to do? Traffic is heavy. People must be leaving work. Maybe I should just return to my room and think of something else.

I closed my eyes, took a deep breath, and decided to give it one last try before turning around and heading home.

My eyes popped open.

Where is home?

I turned left—going the wrong way on a one-way street.

Panic!

I'm on the wrong side of the road. What do I do now?

A car coming straight toward me honked its horn and swerved around, missing my brand-new automobile by inches. I braked. My head jolted forward and back as the oncoming vehicle passed. After I shifted the gear into park, my body convulsed into shivers. I closed my eyes and shook.

No one is hurt. Everything's all right. Get hold of yourself.
Moments passed before a sound startled me.
Tap. Tap.
I turned my head to the left and rolled down the window. "Yes, officer?" I squeaked.

"Do you know you are parked on the wrong side of the road?"

"Oh, please, could you help me?" I blubbered. Tears streamed down my face. My hands shook. I didn't know what to do. "I'm lost. I don't know where to go."

"Okay, tell you what," the officer said. "Just pull the car into the parking lot, and I'll see what I can do."

Traffic had already stopped. I reversed into the parking lot from which I had come earlier.

After checking my license, the policeman, who was not much older than I, agreed to lead me to the packing plant so I could purchase the next morning's lesson. He also drew a map to help me find my way home.

This concluded my first foray into driving around an unfamiliar town and my first run-in with the law.

The following morning, I remembered that science—in this case, biology—lab lessons needed equipment. I stuffed a butcher knife, a sharp steak knife, a metal cookie sheet, and paper towels into my backpack along with the cow's heart, which was still wrapped in butcher paper.

All my twenty-one bright-eyed, nine-year-old students sat or stood around our wooden experiment table as I laid out each item for our science lab. Mrs. Hinckley raised her head high as she watched me take the knives out of my backpack and place them on the table. She said nothing.

"Today, we're going to become laboratory scientists," I told the children. "We're going to dissect a real heart."

Mrs. Hinckley's eyes got big. So did the kids'. While unwrapping the butcher paper, I noticed a dark red, sticky liquid leaking from the paper onto the metal cookie sheet. My teeth clenched. *Oh, no. This heart's full of blood.*

The boys strained forward to get a better look while several girls yelled, moving toward the back. Sharon appeared the most shaken. If a black girl could turn white, she did.

Sharon screamed.

I need to dispose of this heart and blood quickly—before I can deal with Sharon.

My own heart pumped as I hurried into action. Swiftly, I bundled the heart back into its butcher paper wrapper, stuffed it into my backpack, threw paper towels over the spattered cookie sheet, and wiped my hands.

Walking toward Sharon, I announced, "Boys and girls, please return to your places."

"Honey," I said, lowering my voice, "it's gone now. There's no more blood. It's just a cow's heart. I bought it at the meat plant yesterday." I didn't touch Sharon. I suspected she would freak out if I did since the blood had stained my hands.

"We'll go out to get some water and then return to our lesson. I won't use the cow's heart, but we'll talk about how our hearts work instead." Sharon and the other girls calmed down.

Beginning from the first day in Mrs. Hinckley's class and continuing through many more that followed, I discovered I enjoyed working with children. Every day presented interesting and unexpected lessons for both my students and me. Now and then, three girls who walked to school together brought flowers they had picked from the weeds growing along the way. They and I pressed their tokens of love and respect between the pages of my textbooks.

Several weeks into the semester, two girls, one on each side, looked quizzically at my face. "Are you sick?" one asked.

I smiled at the pair. "No, I'm not. Why?"

They giggled, pointed, and said, "You have red spots on your face."

"Those are called acne. I ran out of the makeup that covers them."

"My sister has that, but her spots are black," one girl said.

All through the spring semester, I drove my Chevy the two hours it took back and forth from Shreveport to Fort Polk, driving at a whopping sixty miles per hour, singing the biggest 1960s radio hits all the way.

Aside from student teaching in Shreveport, I labored at home with my parents making plans for my May wedding. We mailed announcements, received gifts, and wrote thank-you notes. The white satin gown and veil my mother designed and sewed fit perfectly. We confirmed arrangements at the post chapel for the ceremony and at the Officers Club for the reception.

But where was the groom?

No letter, card, or phone call had come from my fiancé in several weeks.

I told myself that James, while training at Camp Lejeune, had probably received orders to join the war in Vietnam. *But still—we planned to be married before he leaves. He should have called.*

With our wedding date fast approaching and no word from James, I asked my father if he could do something to find out what had happened. He called the marine command at Camp Lejeune and spoke with the contact there. Dad handed me the phone as soon as James answered. Then my father stepped into the kitchen to give me some privacy.

After taking a steady breath, I said, "James, I haven't heard from you in a while."

"I know. It's been hard." He sounded tired.

"Our wedding is scheduled in two weeks, right after graduation. Is everything okay?"

He seemed to take a long time answering.

"I asked for permission to marry you."

"And?"

"I asked my sergeant, but he said if I needed a wife, they would have requisitioned one for me." Then he sighed. "I didn't know how to tell you."

I felt my heart palpitate faster, but I managed to remain calm. "So, you chose not to tell me?"

Our conversation continued for about five minutes before he said, "I have to hang up now."

That night, after preparing for my return to Shreveport and ruminating over the phone call, I decided, as always, that orders are orders. Not knowing James had to ask permission—and not being given that permission—sounded military enough for me. But the fact that he had not mentioned this in his letters or called to let me know hardened like a clot in the back of my brain. *Have I made a mistake with this man?*

Still engaged but with a house full of gifts to return, I spent my weekends at Fort Polk. With my mother's assistance, we returned the wedding gifts and sent notifications for its cancellation. On the weekend of graduation, my family watched me walk down the aisle and receive my diploma—the first of my entire family to graduate from college.

Graduation from Northwestern State College,
Natchitoches, Louisiana, 1969 –
Mommy, Peggy, and Daddy

As a new Northwestern State College graduate, I had signed a contract committing to teach in a school in Wisconsin during the next academic year. I'd planned to be married to James by then, but while he served in Vietnam, I intended to work where I could enjoy snow again. In the meantime, upon my return from Natchitoches to Fort Polk, a friend of my father's hired me as the summer concierge at the Officers Club. Aside from planning parties, luncheons, and formal affairs, I acted as the cashier in the bar during lunch hours.

Dad often invited the captain who sold my father the Hillman last Christmas to our house for dinner. He had served in the same outfit as Dad in Vietnam—albeit in different places—and had become a friend of the family by then. He even led my brother's Boy Scout troop. I knew him as Joel, and he often sat with me in the bar at the Officers Club while eating his sandwich at lunchtime.

Joel became like a brother. He teased me out of seriousness and listened when I expressed doubts. Often, I ranted about my fiancé and our spoiled plans for marriage. Joel talked about his hopes. He didn't dwell in the past. He looked toward positive outcomes.

"It's getting close to dinnertime," Joel said one evening after a party I planned. "Would you like to go to dinner?"

"I'm engaged."

"It's not a date—just dinner," he said.

We sat opposite each other in the dining area of the Fort Polk Officers Club. Joel's clear, bright blue eyes sparkled like diamonds or like a flash of sun on the Caribbean Sea. His blond crew cut sat a smidgen high on his forehead. His pinkish mouth turned up on one side the way Elvis Presley's did. Exuding confidence, Joel sat ramrod straight. Whenever he looked at me, I could tell he liked what he saw.

I talked about James and the fact that I wanted a career, a marriage, and children. "What do you want?" I asked.

Taking his time, Joel mentioned he was going to Texas A&M to finish his bachelor of science degree in civil engineering. His two tours in Vietnam with the engineers had solidified his decision. "I'm ready for marriage. I'd like five or six kids."

"That's a lot of children," I said. "What do you think about a woman having a career and being married with children?"

"Fine," he said.

One day in late June, I heard from James' sister, Emily.

"Peggy," she said over the phone, "have you heard from James? He's got leave. We're supposed to meet in Alexandria, but we don't know when he's coming in. I thought he would have contacted you."

Shock.

My heart beat into my throat.

Deep breath.

I managed to keep my cool until after the call ended. Then, I blew up. "He's got leave and didn't call me!" I wanted to throw something at the phone or maybe pitch the telephone through the window.

Dad came to my rescue. "Do you want me to call his headquarters again and see what is really going on?"

I did.

This time, the call was briefer than before.

"Your sister called. She wants to know when you will be in for leave. You need to call her."

"Okay."

"When are you coming to see me?"

"I only have two weeks to spend with my family."

"I would have been your family!"

Silence.

I picked James up at the bus stop on July 3, 1969. He stepped down from the bus carrying one brown leather suitcase. He waved but did not smile while he hefted his duffle bag from the luggage compartment.

I noticed how handsome he looked standing straight and thin. The anxiety and anger I felt after our telephone conversation dissipated. I walked up to him, smiling. We embraced then loaded the car and drove to my parents' home for dinner.

Nobody spoke about our wedding or about James leaving for Vietnam.

An uncomfortable fog of uncertainty hovered between us. Instead of facing our situation, we silently chose to ignore the loss of our plans for marriage, the fact that he may or may not return from war, and the hurt I felt from not being invited to his family gathering.

"We'll go to the Fourth of July picnic on post," I said. "Then, I'll drive you over to Natchitoches so you can go with Emily to Alexandria."

"You don't have to. My mother can come get me," he said.

His mother? I was supposed to be his wife.

The next afternoon, on the Fourth of July, we headed for Northwestern State College. Comfortable in familiar surroundings, we walked the paths we had walked before, discussed our past on campus, and visited with his friends. But when we pulled up to Emily's house, we discovered she and her husband had already left for their reunion—which was to double as James' farewell.

We drove to a nearby Denny's to figure out our next move.

"Why was I not invited to your going-away party?"

"Mother said only family should see me away."

"Your mother doesn't like me."

James said nothing.

"She knows we were to be married. Did she talk you out of it?"

"I'm a marine. I may not come back. You could become a widow. It's better this way."

That thought had never occurred to me. My father served in World War II, Korea, and Vietnam. He returned unharmed. I hadn't met anyone who hadn't returned.

Wake up, Peggy. You see this war on television every night. The daily body bag count means those guys are dead. Mothers, wives, and children are left without their husbands, fathers, and sons. Get real.

But if he loved me, wouldn't he have told me sooner that he couldn't marry? Wouldn't he have told me about the family meeting?

James took my hand over the table. "I have too much on my mind right now," he said. "I've got to stay focused."

It seemed as if a cube of silence had slid over our table and separated us from the crowd. I slipped my engagement ring off my finger and handed it to him. "Take this," I said. "I promise I will not marry until you return."

A promise I didn't keep.

After I returned from the trip to Natchitoches and was no longer engaged, Joel showed up at the Officers Club. Dating commenced. Every Friday happy hour, we listened to music over a cocktail or two. On Saturdays, we usually attended a movie or just sat in his bachelor pad watching television. He met me for lunch every day. There was no time to nurse my anger over spoiled wedding plans.

"I want to visit my college roommate," I said one evening. "Linda attends Louisiana State University in Baton Rouge. Will you take me there?"

On July 20, 1969, we drove to Baton Rouge, where I stayed one night with my roommate and the next with Joel. After attending the theater production *Gypsy,* we watched the lunar landing and the first step on the moon. Neil Armstrong said, "That's one small step for man, one giant leap for mankind." That night was also one step for us, the start of our giant leap, and it was indeed "beautiful, beautiful" as Buzz Aldrin expressed.

Joel and I dated through the first part of August. Since he lived about three blocks away from me in Leesville, he often stopped at my house at the end of the day. Whenever the doorbell rang, I'd look out the window and see him in uniform. As soon as I opened the door, his face lit up with his lopsided smile.

I cannot let this guy go.

I wished I had not committed to a Wisconsin school.

Joel and I have dated less than two months. If I leave, will that end our relationship?

No matter how I felt, a contract was a contract.

I began the school year as a fourth-grade teacher in a high-end area of Racine, Wisconsin. Teaching duties kept me busy, as did settling into my apartment and learning to live with a new roommate. That life lasted only a month before Joel called from Fort Polk.

"Peggy, I have four weeks of leave coming at the end of September. I think I'll be coming up to see you. What do you think about the possibility of getting together forever?"

A smile covered my entire face. *He's asking me to marry him.*

On the dates and outings we'd had since July 5th, we both spoke about our desires to have marriage partners. We had not talked about love—whatever that was—but we enjoyed each other and definitely felt an energy between us. We each knew we were meant to be together. Even though we were separated for a brief time, we sent frequent greeting cards, and he called often. The word *love* didn't cross our lips.

Meanwhile, James went to Vietnam. He sent me a letter within the month after I moved to Wisconsin. Still angry at the way he left me at the altar, I tore the envelope and letter into pieces without opening it and tossed it into the garbage. I knew in my heart that Joel was a better prospect for marriage than was James, but along with my anger, I still had feelings for James and worried about him in Vietnam.

Joel arrived at my apartment on September 13, 1969, two days after my birthday. He got on his knees and asked for my hand in marriage. Then, he placed a white gold promise ring on my finger. Knowing he had to report back to Fort Polk within the month, we took a trip to Des Plaines, Illinois, to visit with my aunt Kathleen. While there, we managed to get our blood tests, wedding license, and engagement and wedding bands. We also spoke with Aunt Kathleen's parish priest, who agreed to marry us in the Catholic church the next weekend.

During the following seven days, Joel stayed with another male friend at the apartment complex and called relatives, announcing our wedding. I taught school during the week, wrote my resignation letter, and received dismissal from the Racine School System.

On Saturday, September 20, 1969, Captain Best married Margaret "Peggy" Greene in a small chapel in Des Plaines, Illinois,

Marriage of Joel Best and Peggy Greene

before my family and his. We then drove, visiting my relatives in New York and both his and mine in Pennsylvania, on our way to our new home in Fort Polk, just like I had during every leave with my parents.

During our first year of marriage, I transitioned from a soldier's daughter to a soldier's wife. A new adventure for this dandelion child was about to begin.

Author's Note

I was a soldier's wife for only three months before my husband decided to take a leave of absence. He remained in the Army Reserves and attended college at Texas A&M. During his time as an Aggie, he spent one weekend each month and two weeks each year training with the reserves. After his graduation in 1973, we debated returning to the service. However, his dream job of working as a civil engineer for a construction company came to fruition. Brown & Root made an offer he couldn't refuse, so we became civilians. For the following fifty years, we remained in the civilian world, though with strong connections to the military.

We moved many times—as we both had during our lives as military brats. We lived in several states and countries before retiring in The Villages, Florida, where we are involved with various veterans' associations, The Vietnam Veterans, The Villages Honor Flight, and Veterans of Foreign Wars.

Our two sons were born in different places in Texas, and our daughter's birth occurred in New Mexico. I taught school wherever we lived, and Joel progressed in his profession working for Brown & Root in Texas and New Mexico, then for Salt River Project in Arizona, and finally for Exxon in Texas, Japan, Egypt, Puerto Rico, Wyoming, Florida, and Guam. He also progressed in rank with the Army Reserves and retired from the service in 1992 with the rank of lieutenant colonel.

As for James, I heard from him by email twenty-one years after we parted. He returned from Vietnam, completed his wildlife degree, stayed in Louisiana, married a woman, and had one daughter. We parted as friends.

In 1992, I finally received a diagnosis for all the fainting I experienced growing up: relapsing-remitting multiple sclerosis. My diagnosis came hard yet also as a relief. I knew there was a reason for my loss of consciousness.

I retired from teaching in 2001. I began writing in earnest and published my first book, *Unsung Hero*, in February 2018. *Unsung Hero* is a memoir/biography/tribute to my father, Major Albert V. Greene, who was a prisoner of war during World War II, served in Korea, and earned his third bronze star with valor in Vietnam.

This book, *Dandelion Child: A Soldier's Daughter,* is my memoir of growing up. Both books can be purchased from Amazon.com.

My husband and I celebrate our fiftieth wedding anniversary in 2019. We will be surrounded by our three adult children, their spouses, and our eight grandchildren. Even though I deal with the stresses and fatigue accompanying a chronic illness and my husband lives with diabetes, hearing loss, and other problems from Agent Orange exposure during the war in Vietnam, life has been good. This dandelion child is grateful she grew up in the military.

You are welcome to contact me at peggy.best47@gmail.com or visit my website at www.PeggyBest.com.

Resources
to Help Military Families

When I was a dandelion child, a soldier's daughter during the Cold War era, there was no help available for military families other than that which they could provide themselves. Today, there are organizations—military, governmental, and civilian—that need our support to help our military families. Please visit the websites of the organizations I have listed here to discover what you can do:

www.OperationWeAreHere.com

Operation We Are Here contains resources to help the military community and its supporters. Here you will find practical insight into how to care for the military community. This interest-based list offers essential information for those who support the military—as well as free thank-you cards available for downloading, printing, and sharing.

After Benita Koeman, the founder of Operation We Are Here, found herself lacking support while her husband was deployed, she created this website to help other service wives as well as to provide tools to help civilians who care about military personnel and their families.

Whether you are on active duty, a family member, or a friend of the military, this website is a good starting place for help in many areas. Resources for teachers and homeschoolers include worksheets, lesson plans, and reading lists. Links to information on a wide range of topics—from PTSD to deployment to veteran care and much more—are also available.

In this dandelion child's opinion, this is the first place to look for information.

https://www.MilitaryFamily.org

In 1969, a group of military wives who gathered over coffee and the kitchen table created an organization to benefit the surviving wives of service members who were killed in action. In time, their efforts grew into the National Military Family Association. The NMFA also welcomes the help of civilians committed to the well-being of service personnel and their families.

Through its Operation Purple, NMFA provides children whose parents have deployed with the opportunity to attend a week-long summer camp at no cost. Operation Purple offers healing retreats for military families as well.

The NMFA also awards scholarships that military spouses can apply toward educational or professional expenses.

Donating to the NMFA is a great way to support members of the military community.

https://www.MilitaryOneSource.mil

The confidential Military OneSource program is both a call center—for immediate supportive consultations by phone or in person—and a website with vast, complete information resources. Funded by the Department of Defense, the Military OneSource site serves active duty service personnel, including reservists and National Guard members—as well as their families and their survivors—at no cost.

Available help addresses areas as varied as spousal and parent-child relationships, deployment and reunion issues, employment and educational needs, grieving and stress management, physical and financial health matters including taxes, and more.

From every part of the world, eligible individuals may access these confidential services at any time—twenty-four hours a day, every day of the year—by telephone as well as online.

https://www.RealWarriors.net

The Real Warriors Campaign, a component of the Department of Defense's plan to further psychological health, is overseen by the Psychological Health Center of Excellence. This organization's purpose includes promoting excellent levels of psychological health care to better the quality of life for military personnel—including current service members as well as veterans—and their families.

The website presents resources to guide parents in aiding dependent children through issues related to deployment. It acknowledges that ages and developmental stages impact children's needs and experiences within their military families.

https://ChildMind.org/our-impact/support-for-military-families/
The nonprofit Child Mind Institute aims to help children receive critically important mental health care. Because of the organization's commitment to supporting military families, the CMI website includes articles and resources specifically chosen to help US military personnel succeed in parenting their children, whose lives include both positive and difficult experiences their nonmilitary peers lack.

Along with other useful information on this site, service families will find help with circumstances ranging from school adjustments because of moves and deployments to dealing with traumas such as a parent's injury or death. The Child Mind Institute's Trauma and Resilience Service can help assess the needs of military children and their families facing such traumatic, stressful circumstances and can provide appropriate, military-minded treatment.

Review Request

Thank you for reading *Dandelion Child*. If you enjoyed it, please post a short review on Amazon.com and email a copy to the author at **peggy.best47@gmail.com**. She would be most grateful because your support helps her with the distribution of this book. She promises to read and consider all feedback provided in writing future books.

Unsung Hero
Margaret Best

This award-winning memoir/biography/tribute contains the true experiences of an American soldier taken prisoner by the German Wehrmacht during World War II. Read and marvel at an ordinary soldier's memories written in his words. His life story, couched within the backdrop of American and world history, invokes the spirit of patriotism, duty, and honor that all unsung heroes display.

The 2018 Royal Palm Literary Award-winning *Unsung Hero* is available on Amazon.com and Lulu.com.

Engage with author Margaret Best at **PeggyBest.com** or **PeggyBestMemoirs.com** or by email at **Peggy.Best47@gmail.com**.

CPSIA information can be obtained
at www.ICGtesting.com
Printed in the USA
FFHW010901101019
55428369-61221FF